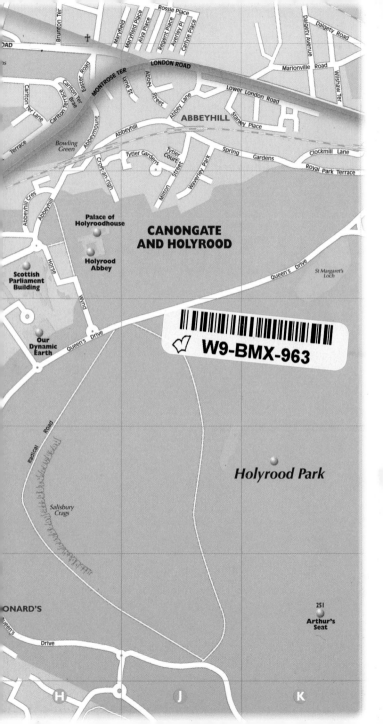

How to Use This Book

KEY TO SYMBOLS

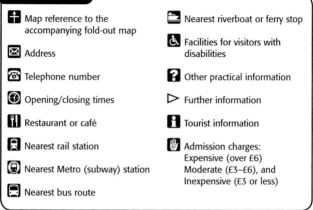

➕ Map reference to the accompanying fold-out map

✉ Address

☎ Telephone number

🕐 Opening/closing times

🍴 Restaurant or café

🚆 Nearest rail station

Ⓜ Nearest Metro (subway) station

🚌 Nearest bus route

🚢 Nearest riverboat or ferry stop

♿ Facilities for visitors with disabilities

❓ Other practical information

▷ Further information

ℹ Tourist information

✋ Admission charges: Expensive (over £6) Moderate (£3–£6), and Inexpensive (£3 or less)

This guide is divided into four sections

• Essential Edinburgh: An introduction to the city and tips on making the most of your stay.

• Edinburgh by Area: We've broken the city into four areas, and recommended the best sights, shops, entertainment venues, nightlife and restaurants in each one. Suggested walks help you to explore on foot.

• Where to Stay: The best hotels, whether you're looking for luxury, budget or something in between.

• Need to Know: The info you need to make your trip run smoothly, including getting about by public transport, weather tips, emergency phone numbers and useful websites.

Navigation In the Edinburgh by Area chapter, we've given each area its own color, which is also used on the locator maps throughout the book and the map on the inside front cover.

Maps The fold-out map accompanying this book is a comprehensive street plan of Edinburgh. The grid on this fold-out map is the same as the grid on the locator maps within the book. We've given grid references within the book for each sight and listing.

Contents

CONTENTS

Introducing Edinburgh

Edinburgh, the striking capital of Scotland, attracts many thousands of visitors every year. They come for many reasons: to seek their ancestral roots, to experience the Festival or just to get a taste of what makes Scotland tick.

Few first-time visitors are prepared for the sheer majesty of the city and the richness of its history and culture. Edinburgh combines its past with all that's best in 21st-century life, making it a popular destination and a jumping-off point for exploring Scotland.

Reminders of the past are everywhere. The castle rises over the tall tenements, narrow streets and dark *vennels* (alleyways) of the Old Town, while, to the north, the broad streets and spacious squares of the New Town are lined with gracious 18th-century buildings. Look closer, though, and it becomes clear that the city is no time warp, a tourist hub existing as a living museum or theme park of the Enlightenment.

Scottish monarchs lived in Edinburgh as early as the 11th century, but the city did not become the royal capital until the reign of King James II (*r.* 1437–60). Political power moved to London with the Act of Union in 1707, but the Scotland Act of 1998 created a devolved Scottish Parliament, sitting in a dramatic building at Holyrood. The economy is dominated by the service sector, with the emphasis on financial services, which has encouraged growing numbers of young, ambitious, highly paid professionals. It's these people, rather than the visitors, who have charged the city's renaissance, turning the capital into a slick and stylish metropolis, whose quality of life is rated among the highest in the UK.

Take time to participate in some of the pleasures enjoyed by local people—plays, music, bar-hopping and the club scene—rather than a steady diet of tartan-obsessed Caledonian entertainment.

Facts + Figures

- The population of Edinburgh is around half a million. This swells to more than one million during the Festival in August.
- Together, Edinburgh's Old Town and New Town contain more than 4,500 listed buildings.
- The highest point is Arthur's Seat.

DID YOU KNOW?

Edinburgh was the first city in the world to have a municipal fire service. It was founded in 1824 by local man James Braidwood (1800–1861), who was recognized for his heroism in tackling the raging fires of that year (▷ 125). He later moved to London, forming the precursor to the London Fire Brigade, but was killed in the Tooley Street fire.

MILITARY TATTOO

Book early for this one. The spectacle, held on the castle Esplanade with military precision—the swirl of the kilts, the sound of the pipes—is the greatest tattoo of them all (tickets: ☎ 0131 225 1188; www.edin tattoo.co.uk). It takes place for three weeks in August. At other times of the year, get an insight at the visitor center.

FESTIVAL TIME

Edinburgh's Festival is not one event but many, running concurrently in August. The most prestigious is the Edinburgh International Festival, founded in 1947, which showcases world-class performing arts events. Side by side with this heavy-weight, the anarchic and vast Fringe has plays, music, comedy and dance in nearly 300 venues.

A Short Stay in Edinburgh

DAY 1

Morning Most popular is a stroll down the **Royal Mile** (▷ 28–29). Those who don't want to walk can take the **hop-on-hop-off bus** (▷ 119) to visit the major sights. Get to **Edinburgh Castle** (▷ 24–25) at opening time to avoid the crowds. Close by is the **Tartan Weaving Mill** (▷ 35) and the **Camera Obscura** (▷ 32). Take a bit of time to explore the alleyways (*vennels* and *wynds*) as you walk away from the castle along Castlehill.

Mid-morning Take a look on the right at Victoria Street, with its specialist shops. If you want to walk farther, continue onto West Bow and out into the attractive **Grassmarket** (▷ 32–33), with lots of opportunities for coffee. Retrace your steps and continue along the Royal Mile into Lawnmarket and along to High Street. Take a look at **St. Giles' Cathedral** (▷ 30).

Lunch Have lunch at **The Mitre** (▷ 43), diagonally opposite the Tron.

Afternoon Continue on High Street, where you will find the **Museum of Childhood** (▷ 54–55) and **John Knox House** (▷ 60) opposite. Continue onto Canongate, with the **Museum of Edinburgh** (▷ 53) on the right and **Canongate Tolbooth** (▷ 50–51) on the left. As you near the end of the road you will see the dramatic **Scottish Parliament Building** (▷ 57) on the right and shortly afterwards the **Palace of Holyroodhouse** (▷ 58–59).

Dinner For old-fashioned charm at a price try the **Witchery by the Castle** (▷ 44). For a taste of France, head for **Petit Paris** (▷ 44).

Evening Just to the west of the Old Town you will find **Usher Hall** (▷ 41), where you can take in a classical concert. If clubbing is more your thing, try **Espionage** (▷ 40).

DAY 2

Morning Start at the Waverley Station end of **Princes Street** (▷ 74). You can then decide if you want to explore the shops along the famous road or those behind it. Those preferring art can visit the **Scottish National Gallery** (▷ 70–71), just beyond the **Scott Monument** (▷ 76). It is possible to take the free link bus from here to the other galleries.

Mid-morning Have a coffee at the gallery or try the **Forth Floor Restaurant** (▷ 84, panel) at Harvey Nichols, on **Multrees Walk** (▷ 79, panel), just to the north of Princes Street. You can then explore the other designer shops on The Walk.

Lunch Take a pub lunch on Rose Street, which once boasted the most pubs of any street in Edinburgh. The **Mussel Inn** (▷ 86) is a good choice for seafood lovers.

Afternoon Catch a bus from Princes Street out to **Leith** (▷ 94–95) and visit the **Royal Yacht *Britannia*** (▷ 97) and the **Ocean Terminal Centre** (▷ 104). Take a walk along The Shore, with its trendy bars and smart restaurants.

Dinner Back in New Town, eat on the popular George Street. Try the Italian **Gusto** (▷ 85) or, for smart dining, the **Dome** (▷ 84).

Evening Still on George Street, try the most fashionable clubs **Lulu** (▷ 83) or **Shanghai** (▷ 83) in the boutique hotels Tigerlily and Le Monde. Try the Omni Centre at Greenside Place on Leith Street for cinema or a comedy show, or the **Edinburgh Playhouse** (▷ 82), a former cinema and now a multi-purpose auditorium, for musicals, dance or rock concerts.

▶ ▶ ▶

Arthur's Seat ▷ 48–49
Looming above the city, this hill, an extinct volcano, is some 325 million years old.

Calton Hill ▷ 68 This hill in the city center is crowned by a collection of historic monuments.

Canongate Tolbooth ▷ 50–51 This attractive building houses a museum of everyday life.

Scottish Parliament Building ▷ 57
Controversial, expensive, but certainly striking, this building opened in 2004.

Scottish National Gallery of Modern Art ▷ 98 The place to view 20th-century Scottish art and sculpture.

Scottish National Gallery ▷ 70–71 A breathtaking collection of artistic masterpieces.

Scotch Whisky Experience ▷ 31 Your chance to learn more about Scotland's national drink and to taste a wee dram.

St. Giles' Cathedral ▷ 30
This imposing church, dedicated to Edinburgh's patron saint, became a cathedral in the 17th century.

Royal Yacht *Britannia* ▷ 97 All aboard the most famous of ships—a must for royal buffs.

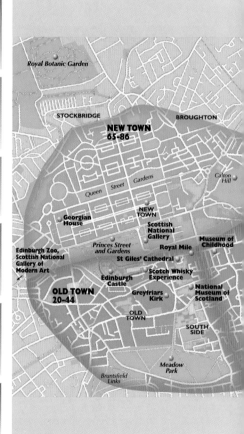

Royal Mile ▷ 28–29
The straight road all the way from Edinburgh Castle to the Palace of Holyroodhouse.

Royal Botanic Garden ▷ 96 A green oasis in a busy capital—there's year-round interest here.

Princes Street and Gardens ▷ 74 After shopping in this famous street, relax in the gardens.

These pages are a quick guide to the Top 25, which are described in more detail later. Here they are listed alphabetically, and the tinted background shows which area they are in.

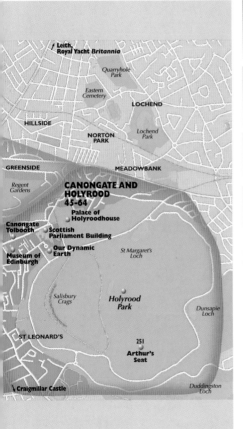

Shopping

Once overshadowed by the glitz of the city of Glasgow, Edinburgh has now won serious shoppers from all over Scotland, as well as countless visitors. Explore by foot to find the best of Scotland on offer.

Get Off the Beaten Track

Shops on Princes Street may be little more than a string of high-street names, and malls ring the suburbs, but away from these Edinburgh offers some of the best shopping in Europe. International names contrast with specialist outlets offering the best of Scottish products, and the goods and service of traditional retailers are hard to find elsewhere. These temples to commerce are housed in a wonderful variety of buildings, ranging from stolid Victorian respectability and glass-and-steel modernity to idiosyncratic individual shops with a quirky charm all their own. The tip is to get off the main drags, away from the crowds, and onto the side streets and alleyways to see everything from custom-made bagpipes to cashmere as soft as a cloud.

Made in Scotland

If you're looking for something typically Scottish, you'll be spoiled for choice whatever your budget. Woolens, tartans, tweeds and cashmeres are everywhere, and smaller stores sell designer knitted goods in rainbow hues, or tartan with a twist, bringing Scottish style right into the 21st century. Tartan can be found in the

From traditional to wacky, designer to vintage— Edinburgh has it all

---

MARKETS

Sunday sees thousands of locals heading out to Ingliston, which is home to a huge, cheap and vibrant outdoor market with more than 100 stands and a car boot sale thrown in. Undercover markets include the rambling New Street Sunday Market in Old Town. For the best in Scottish produce, the Saturday Farmers' Market (9–2), held on Castle Terrace, is worth a trawl for superb organic meat, vegetables and other foods (www.edinburghfarmersmarket.co.uk).

form of everything from a blanket to a kilt. Local craftspeople are celebrated for their silver, metalwork and jewelry, and you'll find samples at the swanky city stores or among dozens of tiny studio-workshops. You can find the country's musical heritage in a huge range of CDs—everything from reels and pipe-and-drum music to Celtic rock and traditional Gaelic song. Books, posters and calendars make great souvenirs and gifts, and you'll find an excellent selection in many book and gift shops. As a capital city, Edinburgh is also well endowed with expensive antiques shops and fine art and contemporary galleries, while other shops specialize in historic maps and antiquarian books with a Scottish theme. Urban sophisticates can bypass all this to focus on furniture and objets d'art that combine traditional craftsmanship with cutting-edge design, not just from Scotland but also from all over the world.

A Taste of Scotland

Food is always a popular souvenir, and shops sell the best of the country's produce, often vacuum-packed to make transportation easier. Choose from wild smoked salmon, Orkney cheese, heather honey and soft fruit jam, shortbread, oatcakes, superb cheeses and a bottle of finest malt whisky from the huge range you'll find—some of which are 100 years old.

SHOPPING AREAS

The city's retail heart beats in Princes Street, and if you're looking for chain stores it's the best choice; if not, with the exception of the excellent department store Jenners, it can be avoided. For souvenirs, head for the Old Town, where tartan, tat, sweaters and whisky crowd the shelves. The New Town's best shops are around Queen Street, with big-name, classy shopping at Multrees Walk (▷ 79) off St. Andrew's Square—home to the beautiful Harvey Nichols. For good local shops, head for Stockbridge, Bruntsfield and Morningside. For style, William Street, in the city's West End, has some great specialist shops.

Eating Out

The culinary explorer is spoiled for choice in cosmopolitan Edinburgh. You don't have to look hard for traditional Scottish cuisine, but there are plenty of alternatives to be found, from Thai and Indian to Turkish and Moroccan.

Where and When to Eat
Restaurants reflect the diversity of British culture and there are options to suit most tastes and pockets. Some of the city's more formal restaurants are open only for lunch and dinner, but you can find somewhere to eat in Edinburgh at almost any time between around midday and midnight and even later. Many city center pubs serve unpretentious, decent meals all day. Many top restaurants are based in hotels, but you need not be staying at the hotel to enjoy the cuisine, although it is best to book in advance. Traditional tea shops are excellent for snacks and are usually open from mid-morning until 4 or 5pm. There are some good options in the larger department stores for light lunches and tea and coffee breaks.

International Dining
Ambitious, innovative cooking based on locally sourced produce and traditional recipes is easy to find, but Edinburgh also offers a good range of international restaurants, including long-established Italian trattorias. With the influx of Italian immigrants to Scotland in the early 20th century, you will find good pasta and, of course, the quintessential Italian-made ice cream.

Eating alfresco is catching on in Britain, even in this northern city

---

SCOTTISH SELECTION

Arbroath smokies—small hot-smoked haddock.
clootie dumpling—steamed sweet-and-spicy pudding, traditionally cooked in a cloth.
cranachan—raspberries, cream and toasted oatmeal.
crowdie—light curd cheese.
Cullen skink—creamy fish broth based on "Finnan haddie," or smoked haddock.
Forfar bridie—pasty made with beef, onion and potato.

Restaurants by Cuisine

There are restaurants to suit all tastes and budgets in Edinburgh. On this page they are listed by cuisine. For a more detailed description of each restaurant, see Edinburgh by Area.

BISTROS/BRASSERIES

Bell's Diner (▷ 84)
Bistro Moderne (▷ 84)
The Canon's Gait (▷ 64)
The Dogs (▷ 84)
Dome (▷ 84)
Doric Tavern (▷ 84)
Earthy Canonmills
    (▷ 85)
Edinburgh Larder (▷ 42)
Hadrian's Brasserie
    (▷ 85)
North Bridge Brasserie
    (▷ 43)
The Scran and Scallie (▷ 86)
Smoke Stack (▷ 86)
Whiski Rooms (▷ 44)

FINE DINING

Number One (▷ 86)
Restaurant at the Bonham
    (▷ 106)
Rhubarb (▷ 106)

FISH/SEAFOOD

A Room in Leith (▷ 106)
Mussel Inn (▷ 86)
Ondine (▷ 44)
Ship on the Shore
    (▷ 106)
Shore Bar & Restaurant
    (▷ 106)

INTERNATIONAL

Le Café St. Honoré
    (▷ 84)
Contini Ristorante (▷ 84)
La Garrigue (▷ 85)
Gusto (▷ 85)
Hanam's (▷ 43)
Kweilin (▷ 85)
The Living Room (▷ 86)
Pancho Villas (▷ 64)
Petit Paris (▷ 44)
La P'tite Folie (▷ 86)
Restaurant Martin Wishart
    (▷ 106)
The Spice Pavilion
    (▷ 86)
VinCaffè (▷ 86)

SCOTTISH CUISINE

Amber Restaurant
    (▷ 42)
Angels with Bagpipes
    (▷ 42)
Deacon Brodie's Tavern
    (▷ 42)
Dubh Prais Restaurant
    (▷ 64)
Grain Store (▷ 43)
Howies (▷ 85)
The Mitre (▷ 43)

Monteiths (▷ 43)
One Square (▷ 44)
Tower Restaurant (▷ 44)
Witchery by the Castle
    (▷ 44)

SNACKS/LIGHT BITES

Bennets Bar (▷ 42)
Elephant House (▷ 42)
Mums (▷ 43)
Oink (▷ 43)
Olive Branch (▷ 86)
Starbank Inn (▷ 106)

VEGETARIAN

David Bann's Vegetarian
    Restaurant (▷ 64,
    panel)
Henderson's Salad Table
    (▷ 85)

Top Tips For...

However you'd like to spend your time in Edinburgh, these top suggestions should help you tailor your ideal visit. Each sight or listing has a fuller write-up elsewhere in the book.

SCOTTISH SOUVENIRS

Kilts and all things tartan can be found at Geoffrey Kiltmakers (▷ 62) and their Tartan Weaving Mill (▷ 35).

Scottish pipes and music are sold at Bagpipes Galore (▷ 62).

Try a wee dram—there's a huge choice of Scotland's national tipple (drink) at Royal Mile Whiskies (▷ 39).

See the work of local craftspeople at Just Scottish (▷ 39).

For quality reproductions of prints, paintings, jewelry and other relics from the collections held in Edinburgh's great museums and art galleries, visit the shops in the National Museum of Scotland, the Scottish National Portrait Gallery or the National Library of Scotland.

Superior malt whisky makes a great gift

LUXURIOUS CASHMERE

Belinda Robertson (▷ 78) produces designer cashmere products to dress the stars.

For the very best quality shop at the Hawick Cashmere Company (▷ 38), but it will cost.

SCOTTISH FOOD

Enjoy top dining and Scottish classics with a contemporary twist at the Witchery (▷ 44).

Sample top Scottish cuisine at Dubh Prais Restaurant (▷ 64), with everything from haggis to salmon.

Try the Whiski Rooms (▷ 44) on the Royal Mile for hundreds of malt whiskies and a menu that emphasizes locally produced meat, game and seafood.

A taste of luxury, be it supersoft cashmere (middle) or delicious locally caught salmon (bottom)

When the weather's good, eat outside or take to the hills

INTERNATIONAL COOKING

Cool, sleek and Italian is the dish of the day at Gusto (▷ 85).

French cuisine in Grassmarket—try a delightful country-style bistro in the heart of the city at Petit Paris (▷ 44).

Dine on fresh seafood at the Mussel Inn (▷ 86), simply prepared and a delight to the taste buds.

A taste of Mexico can be found at Pancho Villas (▷ 64) in Canongate.

A BREATH OF FRESH AIR

Classical Edinburgh can be found at the top of Calton Hill (▷ 68).

For some salty air head out to Leith (▷ 94–95) and go aboard the Royal Yacht *Britannia* (▷ 97).

In the heart of the city stroll in the delightful Princes Street Gardens (▷ 74).

If you are feeling energetic get down to Holyrood Park (▷ 52) and climb up to Arthur's Seat (▷ 48–49).

BOUTIQUE HOTELS

From Paris to Marrakesh—stay in a global suite at the fabulous Le Monde (▷ 111).

Enjoy spectacular views of Calton Hill from the comfort of your bedroom at the Glasshouse (▷ 112).

Walking the dog on Calton Hill

One of the coolest hotels in town is The Bonham (▷ 112), nicely located in New Town.

True elegance and sophistication can be found at The Howard (▷ 112).

Relax in one of Edinburgh's newest boutique hotels

TO SAVE SOME MONEY

Attractions in the city range from art to animals

Stay in a hostel like the one in Belford Road (▷ 109).
Buy the Edinburgh Pass (▷ 119) if you want to see the attractions.
Picnic in the park at Holyrood (▷ 52) and save your lunch money.
Visit the Scottish National Gallery (▷ 70–71)—it's free and packed with great art.

A KID'S DAY OUT

See the animals at the world-renowned zoo (▷ 92–93).
Give yourself a scare in the Edinburgh Dungeon (▷ 75).
It's free at the Museum of Childhood (▷ 54–55).
Be hands-on and scientific at the terrific Our Dynamic Earth (▷ 56).

SOME ACTION

Play a round of golf just outside the city (▷ 105, panel).
Enjoy a swim at the Royal Commonwealth Pool (▷ 105).
See Scottish football at Hearts or Hibs (▷ 105).
Spend a day at the races—check out the horses at Musselburgh Racecourse (▷ 105).

The game of golf began in Scotland

GOING OUT ON THE TOWN

Traditional music can be found at Sandy Bells Bar (▷ 40, panel).
Go clubbing at Lulu (▷ 83), in the Tigerlily hotel.
Boogie all night down at club Espionage (▷ 40).
Some great jazz, soul and blues bands appear at The Jazz Bar (▷ 64).

Take to the dance floor

Edinburgh by Area

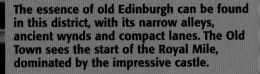

The essence of old Edinburgh can be found in this district, with its narrow alleys, ancient wynds and compact lanes. The Old Town sees the start of the Royal Mile, dominated by the impressive castle.

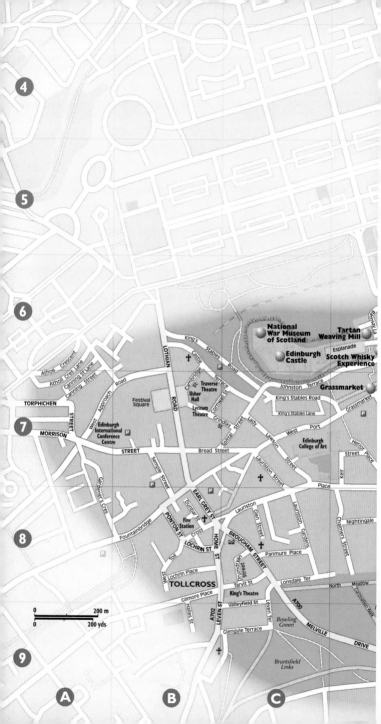

4

5

6

National
War Museum
of Scotland

Tartan
Weaving Mill

King's

Stables

Road

Castle

Terrace

Cambridge St

Traverse
Theatre

Usher
Hall

Cornwall St

Lyceum
Theatre

Grindlay

St

Spittal Street

Lady

Lawson

West

Port

LOTHIAN

ROAD

Edinburgh
Castle

Scotch Whisky
Experience

Esplanade

Johnston Terrace

King's Stables Road

King's Stables Lane

Grassmarket

Grassmarket

West
Approach
Road

Canning Street

Canning St Lane

Atholl Cres Lane

Atholl Crescent

Festival
Square

TORPHICHEN

7 MORRISON

STREET

Edinburgh
International
Conference
Centre

STREET

Bread Street

Lauriston

Street

Edinburgh
College of Art

Herlot

Place

Keir

Street

Place

Street

Gardener's Cres

Semple Street

P

Fountainbridge

PONTON ST

EARL GREY ST

Dunbar St

HOME ST

Fire
Station

Cross

LOCHRIN ST

West

Toll

Lochrin Place

Laurlston

Glen Street

BROUGHAM STREET

Drumdryan Street

Panmure Place

Lauriston Gardens

Chalmers Street

Nightingale

North

Meadow

8

P

P

Lonsdale Ter

TOLLCROSS

Tarvit St

King's Theatre

Gilmore Place

Valleyfield St

Leven St

A700

Bowling
Green

MELVILLE

DRIVE

Home Street

A702

LEVEN ST

Glengyle Terrace

Bruntsfield
Links

Crossway Walk

0   200 m

0   200 yds

9

A   **B**   **C**

The Real Mary
King's Close
The
Writers'
Museum
Gladstone's
Land
Mercat
Cross
Royal
Mile
The Mound
Lawnmarket
High St
Cockburn St.
Camera
Obscura
& World
of Illusions
Heart of
Midlothian
St Giles' Cathedral
Charles II
Statue
Parliament House
Blair St.
SOUTH BRIDGE
Victoria St
George IV Bridge
Candlemaker Row
National
Library of
Scotland
Cowgate
Guthrie St.
Melbourne Place
Market Bridge
OLD
TOWN
University of
Edinburgh Old College
Talbot Rice
Gallery
NICOLSON STREET
Greyfriars
Kirk
Forrest Rd
Bristo Place
Chambers Street
National
Museum of
Scotland
Festival
Theatre
Potterrow
Nicolson
Square
Bedlam
Theatre
Teviot Pl
Bristo
Square
Windmill
Street
Mosque
West Nicolson
Street
Lauriston Place
University of
Edinburgh
Chapel Street
CLERK STREET
Way
George Square
SOUTH
SIDE
George Square
Gardens
University of
Edinburgh
St Patrick St.
Simpson Loan
George Square
Buccleuch Place
Buccleuch Street
Gifford Place
Walk
George Square Lane
Meadow Lane
Meadow Park
Jawbone Walk
Middle Meadow Walk
Boys Brigade Walk
Tennis
Courts
Hope
Park Ter.
SOUTH CLERK STREET
SUMMERHILL PLACE
MELVILLE DRIVE
A700

D   E   F   G

Edinburgh Castle

HIGHLIGHTS

- Great views
- St. Margaret's Chapel
- Mons Meg
- Prisons of War Exhibition
- Scottish Crown Jewels
- Stone of Destiny
- Scottish War Memorial
- One O'Clock Gun

TIP

- The nearest car parking zones are at Castle Terrace and Johnson Terrace. Visitors with disabilities can arrange to park at the castle.

Perched high on a wedge of volcanic rock, the castle is a symbol of the Scottish nation, reflecting 1,000 years of history and displaying a rich mix of architectural styles.

Might and majesty As you wind your way up the Castle Rock you can enjoy the view north over the city. The cannons along the battery were a picturesque improvement suggested by Queen Victoria. The One O'Clock Gun, a 25-pounder field gun from World War II, fires from Mills Mount Battery at precisely 1pm in a tradition dating from 1861. To enter the castle you first cross the Esplanade, the setting for the annual Military Tattoo.

Once inside The oldest structure in the castle is the 12th-century chapel, dedicated to St. Margaret by her son, King David I. The chapel is almost

Clockwise from far left: full military pageant at the annual Edinburgh Tattoo, staged at the castle; stained-glass window depicting Queen Margaret inside St. Margaret's Chapel; the proud fortress overlooks the city; St. Margaret's Chapel; bands at the Tattoo; Mons Meg cannon on the ramparts

overshadowed by the huge cannon on the rampart outside—Mons Meg, a gift in 1457 to James II from the Duke of Burgundy.

Castle of contrasts One of the newest build-ings on Castle Rock is the austere National War Memorial. Be prepared for crowds in the Crown Room, where the Scottish Crown Jewels and the Stone of Destiny are displayed. The crown, dat-ing from 1540, is made of Scottish gold, studded with semi-precious stones from the Cairngorms. The sword and sceptre were papal gifts. The Stone of Destiny was the stone on which Scottish kings were crowned—pinched by Edward I, it was recovered from London's Westminster Abbey in 1996. The castle also contains the National War Museum of Scotland (▷ 34) and the Prisons of War Exhibition.

THE BASICS

www.edinburghcastle.gov.uk

✚ C6

✉ Castlehill EH1 2NG

☎ 0131 225 9846

🕐 Apr–Sep daily 9.30–6; Oct–Mar daily 9.30–5

🍴 Cafés

🚌 23, 27, 41, 42

🚉 Edinburgh Waverley

♿ Some areas are restricted; call first. A courtesy minibus takes less mobile people to the top of the castle site—check when you buy your ticket

💰 Expensive

Greyfriars Kirk

The loyal Greyfriars Bobby sits patiently outside the church and graveyard

THE BASICS

www.greyfriarskirk.com
🕇 E7
✉ Greyfriars Tolbooth and Highland Kirk, Greyfriars Place EH1 2QQ
☎ 0131 225 1900
🕐 Apr–Oct Mon–Fri 10.30–4.30, Sat 10.30–2.30; Nov–Mar Thu 1.30–3.30
🚍 2, 23, 27, 35, 41, 42
🚉 Edinburgh Waverley
♿ Very good
🎫 Free

HIGHLIGHTS

● Greyfriars Bobby
● Elaborate 17th-century memorials
● Peaceful surroundings
● Gaelic service held at 12.30 on Sunday, when all are welcome

Built in 1620 on the site of the garden of a former Franciscan monastery, the Kirk of the Grey Friars has had a turbulent history. Today it is a peaceful haven for quiet contemplation.

Battleground Just 18 years after the church was built, it was the scene of a pivotal event in Scottish history, when Calvinist petitioners gathered to sign the National Covenant, an act of defiance against the king, Charles I. The church itself was trashed by Cromwell's troops in 1650, and later accidentally blown up. In the kirkyard a makeshift prison was erected to house hundreds of Covenanters captured after the battle of Bothwell Bridge in 1679; they were kept here for five dreadful months. Today it is full of elaborate memorials, including the grave of architect William Adam (1689–1748).

Undying loyalty Opposite the churchyard gate stands a popular Edinburgh landmark: a fountain with a bronze statue of a little Skye terrier, which has stood here since 1873. The dog's story was told by American Eleanor Atkinson in her 1912 novel *Greyfriars Bobby*. He was the devoted companion of a local farmer who dined regularly in Greyfriars Place. After his master died, Bobby slept on his grave in the nearby churchyard for 14 years. A later version suggests he was owned by a local policeman, and taken in by local residents when his owner died. There is a portrait of Bobby, painted by John MacLeod in 1867, inside the church.

The striking National Museum of Scotland incorporates the former Royal Museum

National Museum of Scotland

An unashamedly modern castle protects Scotland's national treasures. Designed by Benson & Forsyth, it incorporates the original 18th-century Royal Museum and was opened in 1998.

Much to see Treasures abound in this superb collection, but it can be confusing to find your way around and you won't see it all in one visit. From the basement, work your way up chronologically through history from the earliest beginnings. Check out the section on early people, with its fascinating sculptures by Eduardo Paolozzi decked out in ancient jewels. The museum's floors follow the history of Scotland, through its Gaelic heritage, the impact of Christianity and the Union with England in 1707. Subsequent galleries display associations with culture, industry and emigration, and the impact of the Scottish nation on the world.

The highlights Worth a look are the displays of the Pictish period: vivid relief carvings in stone. Don't miss the Hunterston brooch, dating from around AD700, or the collection of 82 carved chess pieces discovered in the sands of Uig, on Lewis, in 1831; these small 12th-century greyish figures are carved from walrus ivory.

The future The adjacent Royal Museum, which first opened in 1866, reopened after a splendid makeover in 2011 and is now part of the National Museum complex. It houses a wonderfully eclectic collection.

THE BASICS

www.nms.ac.uk
⊞ E7
✉ Chambers Street EH1 1JF
☎ 0300 123 6789
🕐 Daily 10–5
🍴 Tower Restaurant (▷ 44); reservations essential at weekends. Museum Brasserie
🚌 2, 23, 27, 35, 41, 42
♿ Very good
💷 Free; charge for some temporary exhibitions
❓ Check on arrival for times of free daily tours. Free audio guides available in English, Gaelic, French, Spanish, Italian and German

HIGHLIGHTS

- Pictish carvings
- Hunterston brooch
- Lewis chess pieces
- Robbie Burns' pistols
- Eduardo Paolozzi sculptures
- Great views from the roof

Royal Mile

HIGHLIGHTS

- Narrow closes, *wynds* and *vennels* (alleys)
- Tenement houses
- Edinburgh Castle (▷ 24–25)
- Scotch Whisky Experience (▷ 31)
- St. Giles' Cathedral (▷ 30)
- Canongate Kirk (▷ 60)
- Palace of Holyroodhouse (▷ 58–59)

Stretching downhill from Edinburgh Castle to Holyrood Palace, the Royal Mile is a focal point for visitors, who like to explore the narrow *wynds* leading off the main thoroughfare.

Origins of the Mile The Royal Mile is the long, almost straight street leading up the spine of rock on which the Old Town was built. Lined with medieval tenement houses, this part of the city became so overcrowded that a New Town (▷ 72–73) was built in the 18th century. About 60 narrow closes, or *wynds,* lead off between the buildings on either side, with names, such as Fleshmarket, indicating the trades once carried out there.

Down to earth The Scottish Parliament Building (▷ 57) dominates the Holyrood end of the Royal

Clockwise from top left: Deacon Brodie's—a traditional pub on the Royal Mile; tartan for sale at shops along the Mile; striking Old Town houses at the back of the Royal Mile; the official Royal Mile sign; on the Lawnmarket; attractive pub sign for Deacon Brodie's; buildings on Cockburn Street

Mile. From here, the area around Canongate developed into a more practical, working district. You can see a view of the interiors of these old houses at the Museum of Edinburgh (▷ 53). Look for a board outside the Canongate Kirk (church) indicating the famous buried there.

Onward and upward At the crossing of St. Mary's Street and Jeffrey Street you enter High Street. Above the Tron Kirk (▷ 60) the road retains its *setts* (cobbles) and broadens out. After St. Giles' Cathedral (▷ 30), with the Heart of Midlothian (▷ 33) in the cobbles, the street becomes the Lawnmarket, with its fine 16th- and 17th-century tenements, where linen (lawn) was manufactured. The final stretch lies above the Hub (a converted church), as the road narrows on the steep approach to the castle (▷ 24–25).

THE BASICS

♦ C6–H5
✉ The Royal Mile
🚌 23, 27, 35, 41, 42

TIP

● The route has four sections, each with its own identity. You may wish to walk it all in one go or choose to concentrate on one part.

St. Giles' Cathedral

Striking stained glass depicting biblical scenes in St. Giles' Cathedral

THE BASICS

www.stgilescathedral.org.uk

✠ E6

✉ High Street EH1 1RE

☎ 0131 225 9442

🕓 May–Sep Mon–Fri 9–7, Sat 9–5, Sun 1–5; Oct–Apr Mon–Sat 9–5, Sun 1–5 (and for services year-round)

🍴 St. Giles' Cathedral Café

🚌 23, 27, 35, 41, 42

🚆 Edinburgh Waverley

♿ Very good

💷 Free. A donation of £3 is invited

HIGHLIGHTS

● Robert Louis Stevenson memorial
● Window designed by Edward Burne-Jones
● Robert Burns window
● Stained glass
● John Knox statue
● Medieval stonework

Imposing, and its dark stonework somewhat forbidding, the High Kirk of Edinburgh stands near the top of the Royal Mile. It is dedicated to St. Giles, the patron saint of the city.

Origins of the building The columns inside the cathedral that support the 49m (160ft) tower, with its distinctive crown top, are a relic of the 12th-century church that once occupied this site. The tower itself dates from 1495, and the rest of the church from the 15th and 16th centuries. This tower is one of the few remaining examples of 15th-century work to be seen in High Street today. Much of the church has been altered and reworked over subsequent centuries. Don't miss the exquisitely carved 19th-century Thistle Chapel.

Saintly beginnings St. Giles' parish church—it became a cathedral in the mid-17th century—was probably founded by Benedictine followers of Giles. He was a 7th-century hermit (and later abbot and saint) who lived in France, a country with strong ties to Scotland. In 1466, the Preston Aisle of the church was completed, in memory of William Preston, who had acquired the arm bone of the saint in France. This relic disappeared in about 1577, but St. Giles' other arm bone is still in St. Giles' Church, Bruges.

Famous sons Presbyterian reformer John Knox (c.1513–72) became minister here in 1559. You can also see a bronze memorial to writer Robert Louis Stevenson (1850–94), who died in Samoa.

here. Smartened up in recent years, it now has many good shops and eating places, and the ancient White Hart Inn.

➕ D7 ✉ Grassmarket 🚌 2, 35, 41

HEART OF MIDLOTHIAN

With your back to the entrance of St. Giles' Cathedral, move 20 paces forward and slightly to the right, look down and you will see the outline of a heart in the cobblestones. This Heart of Midlothian marks the place of the old Tolbooth prison, where executions took place.

➕ E6 ✉ High Street EH1 1RE 🚌 35, 42

🚇 Edinburgh Waverley

MEADOW PARK

Known as the Meadows, the paths and tree-planted areas make this an ideal place to wander away from the hustle of the city; although not such a good place to be at night. Students from the university, doctors and nurses from the Royal Infirmary and local families all mingle here.

➕ D9 ✉ Meadow Park 🚌 3, 3A, 5, 7, 31

♿ Good

MERCAT CROSS

Located outside St. Giles' Cathedral, the cross was traditionally the chosen location for public declarations, gatherings and executions. The present version, dating from the 1880s, is fashioned on the 17th-century cross. There may have been a cross here since the 12th century.

➕ E6 ✉ High Street 🚌 23, 27, 35, 41, 42

🚇 Edinburgh Waverley

NATIONAL LIBRARY OF SCOTLAND

www.nls.uk

This dignified building houses extensive collections of reference works, maps, fiction and non-fiction by Scottish authors and publishers and hosts a year-round calendar of literary exhibitions. Highlights include the John Murray Archive, a collection of thousands of manuscripts, letters and other documents from authors including Jane Austen,

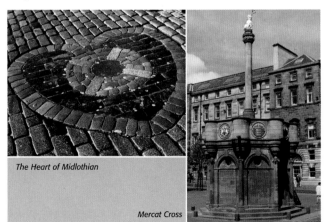

The Heart of Midlothian

Mercat Cross

Lord Byron, Charles Darwin and David Livingstone. The NLS also houses the Scottish Screen Archive, a collection of hundreds of moving images covering more than 100 years of Scottish cinematic history.

➕ E6 ✉ George IV Bridge EH1 1EW ⏰ 0131 623 3700 ⏰ Mon–Fri 10–8, Sat 10–5, Sun 2–5 🚌 23, 27, 41, 42, 67 🚉 Edinburgh Waverley ♿ Good ✋ Free

NATIONAL WAR MUSEUM OF SCOTLAND

www.nms.ac.uk

Exploring more than 400 years of Scottish military history, this museum has displays ranging from major events in Scottish warfare to the personal—diaries, private photographs and belongings of ordinary soldiers. Highlights include a pipe given by a German soldier to a sergeant in the Scots Guards on Christmas Day 1914; weaponry; gallantry medals; and even three elephant's toes.

➕ C6 ✉ Edinburgh Castle, Castle Hill EH1 2NG ⏰ 0131 247 4413 ⏰ Daily

9.45–5.45 (closes 4.45 Nov–Mar) 🚌 23, 27, 41, 42 🚉 Edinburgh Waverly ♿ Good ✋ Expensive (as part of ticket for castle)

PARLIAMENT HOUSE

Home to the law courts, this is the heart of the Scottish legal system. Dating from the 17th century, and restored in 2013, it has a fine hammerbeam roof and a 19th-century stained-glass window. It was home to Parliament from 1639 to 1707 and again from 1999 to 2004.

➕ E6 ✉ Parliament Square EH1 1RF ⏰ 0131 225 2595 ⏰ Mon–Fri 9–5 🚌 23, 27, 35, 41, 42 🚉 Edinburgh Waverley ♿ Good ✋ Free

THE REAL MARY KING'S CLOSE

www.realmarykingsclose.com

Remnants of the Old Town's 17th-century houses have been preserved beneath the City Chamber, which was built over the top in 1753. Guided tours underground bring the close and its people to life.

➕ E6 ✉ 2 Warriston's Close, High Street EH1 1PG ⏰ 0845 070 6244 ⏰ Apr–Oct

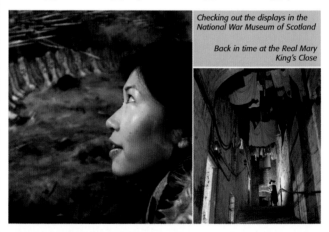

Checking out the displays in the National War Museum of Scotland

Back in time at the Real Mary King's Close

daily 10–9 (Aug 9–9); Nov–Mar Sun–Fri 10–5, Sat 10–9 🚌 23, 27, 35, 41, 42 🚉 Edinburgh Waverley ♿ Few, phone for details 💷 Expensive

TALBOT RICE GALLERY

www.ed.ac.uk/about/museums-galleries/talbot-rice

Within the University of Edinburgh, this gallery was established in 1975 and hosts changing exhibitions showcasing Scottish art and the work of international artists. There is also the fine permanent Torrie collection of Dutch and Italian Old Masters.
➕ E7 ✉ Old College, South Bridge EH8 9YL ☎ 0131 650 2210 🕐 Open only for exhibitions 🚌 3, 7, 8, 14, 33 🚉 Edinburgh Waverley ♿ Good 💷 Free

TARTAN WEAVING MILL

www.geoffreykilts.co.uk/tartanweavingmill.html

From sheep to finished garment, learn about the process of making a kilt—and try the loom. You can buy all manner of highland dress and accessories here, too. There is information about clans and their tartans.
➕ D6 ✉ 555 Castlehill EH1 2ND ☎ 0131 226 1555 🕐 Mon–Sat 9–5.30, Sun 10–5.30 (every day until 6.30 in summer) 🚌 23, 27, 41, 42 🚉 Edinburgh Waverley ♿ Good 💷 Free for exhibition and working looms

THE WRITERS' MUSEUM

www.edinburghmuseums.org.uk

The 17th-century Lady Stair's House is home to The Writers' Museum and dedicated to Robert Burns (1759–96), Sir Walter Scott (1771–1832) and Robert Louis Stevenson (1850–94). Scott and Stevenson were both born in Edinburgh, and studied law at the university. Particularly significant is Stevenson's memorabilia, as he died abroad and there is no other museum dedicated to him. Contemporary Scottish authors are also represented.
➕ D6 ✉ Lady Stair's Close, Lawnmarket, Royal Mile EH1 2PA ☎ 0131 529 4901 🕐 Mon–Sat 10–5; also Sun 12–5 in Aug 🚌 35 🚉 Edinburgh Waverley ♿ Phone for details 💷 Free

Crossing the spectrum—tartan comes in all shades

Robert Burns' memorabilia on display at The Writers' Museum

A Wander Around the Old Town

Take in some of the highlights off the beaten track and get a glimpse of the buildings of the Old Town.

DISTANCE: 2km (1 mile) **ALLOW:** 45 minutes (but more time with stops)

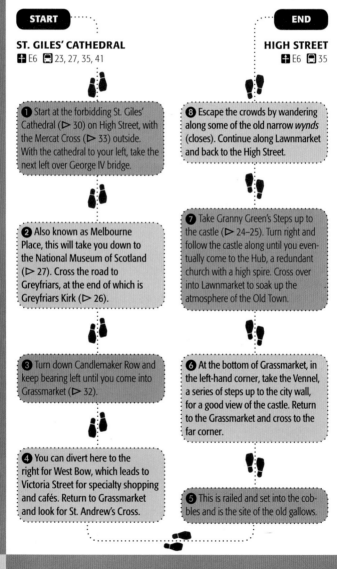

START

ST. GILES' CATHEDRAL
✚ E6 🚌 23, 27, 35, 41

END

HIGH STREET
✚ E6 🚌 35

OLD TOWN WALK

❶ Start at the forbidding St. Giles' Cathedral (▷ 30) on High Street, with the Mercat Cross (▷ 33) outside. With the cathedral to your left, take the next left over George IV bridge.

❷ Also known as Melbourne Place, this will take you down to the National Museum of Scotland (▷ 27). Cross the road to Greyfriars, at the end of which is Greyfriars Kirk (▷ 26).

❸ Turn down Candlemaker Row and keep bearing left until you come into Grassmarket (▷ 32).

❹ You can divert here to the right for West Bow, which leads to Victoria Street for specialty shopping and cafés. Return to Grassmarket and look for St. Andrew's Cross.

❺ This is railed and set into the cobbles and is the site of the old gallows.

❻ At the bottom of Grassmarket, in the left-hand corner, take the Vennel, a series of steps up to the city wall, for a good view of the castle. Return to the Grassmarket and cross to the far corner.

❼ Take Granny Green's Steps up to the castle (▷ 24–25). Turn right and follow the castle along until you eventually come to the Hub, a redundant church with a high spire. Cross over into Lawnmarket to soak up the atmosphere of the Old Town.

❽ Escape the crowds by wandering along some of the old narrow *wynds* (closes). Continue along Lawnmarket and back to the High Street.

Shopping

ANALOGUE
www.analoguebooks.co.uk
A bookshop with a difference that stocks design and contemporary culture books, and also a selection of magazines, music, posters and T-shirts.
🔹 D7 ✉ 39 Candlemaker Row EH1 2QB ☎ 0131 220 0601 🚌 2, 23, 27, 41

ANTA
www.anta.co.uk
Highland-made and designed fabrics, throws and cushions in wool and tweed in trendy and classic tartans. Also stoneware, tiles and luggage.
🔹 B5 ✉ 119 George Street EH2 4JN ☎ 0131 225 9096 🚌 24, 29, 42

ARMSTRONGS
www.armstrongsvintage.co.uk
Established in 1840, museum-like Armstrongs is Scotland's largest vintage emporium, featuring sassy, retro and traditional Scottish clothing. There are also branches at 64–66 Clerk Street and 14 Teviot Place.
🔹 D7 ✉ 83 Grassmarket EH1 2HJ ☎ 0131 220 5557 🚌 2

BILL BABER
www.billbaber.com
Bill Baber and his partner Helen have been creating beautiful garments since 1977, using yarns of raw and blended silk, organic Irish linen and soft Egyptian cotton, as well as merino wool spun and dyed in Milan.
🔹 D7 ✉ 66 Grassmarket EH1 2JR ☎ 0131 225 3249 🚌 2, 23, 27, 41

BLACKWELL
www.bookshop.blackwell.co.uk
This large company, with several branches throughout Edinburgh, has been providing a comprehensive range of books and publications for more than 150 years.
🔹 F7 ✉ 53–62 South Bridge Street EH1 1YS ☎ 0131 622 8222 🚌 3, 5, 7, 14, 29, 30, 31, 33, 37, 49

CIGAR BOX
This Royal Mile retailer has achieved the Gold Standard in Habanos. From famous names like Montecristo and Romeo y Julieta to cigars from as far afield as Honduras and Nicaragua, you'll find them here.

SCOTTISH WOOL
If you're looking for the very best in Scottish woolen items, you could spend a small fortune on designer cashmere in Edinburgh, but equally, you'll find a plethora of factory outlets with good-quality knitwear at knock-down prices, particularly cashmere. However, you are unlikely to find anything leading the way in designer fashion at the mill outlets. Serious knitters will delight in the huge range of yarns available in every conceivable shade, at a good price.

🔹 E6 ✉ 361 High Street EH1 1PW ☎ 0131 225 3534 🚌 35 and North Bridge buses

DEMIJOHN
www.demijohn.co.uk
A liquid deli where you can taste the products and personalize them with your choice of bottle; liqueurs, spirits, whisky, oils, vinegars and spices from around the world.
🔹 D6 ✉ 32 Victoria Street EH1 2JW ☎ 0131 225 4090 🚌 2, 23, 27, 41

FABHATRIX
www.fabhatrix.com
This hat shop promotes Scottish designers and many hats are made on the premises. You'll find everything from tweed to trendy fascinators.
🔹 D7 ✉ 13 Cowgatehead EH1 1JY ☎ 0131 225 9222 🚌 2, 23, 27, 41

HAWICK CASHMERE COMPANY
www.hawickcashmere.com
Cashmere doesn't come cheap and sweaters from this boutique start at £180—the 'Cashmere Made In Scotland' label attached to each garment satisfies that the clothes are of the highest quality. Also sells scarves.
🔹 D7 ✉ 71 Grassmarket EH1 2HJ ☎ 0131 225 8634 🚌 2

HERMAN BROWN
www.hermanbrown.co.uk
Just off Grassmarket, Herman Brown has a wealth of hand-picked vintage clothing and

accessories for men and women.

➕ C7 ✉ 151 West Port EH3 9DP ☎ 0131 228 2589
🚌 23, 27, 41, 42, 67

IAN MELLIS

www.mellischeese.co.uk
Lovers of cheese owe it to themselves to visit this cheesemonger. The range of Scottish cheeses is overwhelming, but staff will help find the perfect cheese for your palate. There are also branches in Morningside and Stockbridge.

➕ D6 ✉ 30a Victoria Street EH1 2JW ☎ 0131 226 6215
🚌 2, 23, 27, 41

JUST SCOTTISH

www.justscottishart.com
An eclectic mix of fine and applied art from the best of Scotland's artists. Choose from zany cushions, traditional ceramics, beautifully crafted wooden items and a selection of cards.

➕ D6 ✉ 4–6 North Bank Street EH1 2LP ☎ 0131 226 4806 (gallery 0131 226 4807)
🚌 3, 3A, 31, 33

K1 YARNS

www.K1yarns.com
Not quite like the knitting shop of granny's day, this boutique sells the best and most beautiful yarns from Scotland and as far away as Japan and South America. The website has details of knitting classes.

➕ D6 ✉ 89 West Bow EH1 2JP ☎ 0131 226 7472 🚌 2, 23, 27, 41

MR WOOD'S FOSSILS

www.mrwoodsfossils.co.uk
This shop originally supplied museums but now specializes in selling fossils, crystals and minerals from Scotland and all over the world. Knowledgeable and friendly staff will fill you in on Lizzie, the oldest reptile ever discovered.

➕ D7 ✉ 5 Cowgatehead EH1 1JY ☎ 0131 220 1344
🚌 2, 23, 27, 41, 42

OLD TOWN BOOKSHOP

www.oldtownbookshop-edinburgh.co.uk
Secondhand books on Scotland and Scottish

writers, plus poetry, music, travel, art and lots more. There is also a wide selection of prints and maps.

➕ D6 ✉ 8 Victoria Street EH1 2HG ☎ 0131 225 9237
🚌 2, 23, 27, 41

RED DOOR GALLERY

www.edinburghart.com
This trendy gallery sells original prints, quirky accessories, jewelry and more. The color red is a recurrent theme here.

➕ D6 ✉ 42 Victoria Street EH1 2JW ☎ 0131 477 3255
🚌 23, 27, 41, 42, 67

ROYAL MILE WHISKIES

www.royalmilewhiskies.com
Enthusiasts are on hand to offer advice on the hundreds of single malt whiskies stocked here—some are 100 years old. Have your items shipped home, or order by phone or online.

➕ E6 ✉ 379 High Street EH1 1PW ☎ 0131 524 9380
🚌 23, 27, 35, 41, 42

TOTTY ROCKS

www.tottyrocks.bigcartel.com
Totty Rocks is primarily an independent womenswear label, but you'll also find items for men and children. The collection is designed upstairs and all pieces are made in Scotland. It's one for the individualist.

➕ B9 ✉ 45–47 Barclay Place EH10 4HW ☎ 0131 229 0474 🚌 23, 27, 41, 42, 67

Entertainment and Nightlife

BOW BAR

If it's a wee dram you're after, this traditional pub is the place for whisky, with more than 140 malts to choose from. Wood panels, old brewery mirrors and a warm greeting create an authentic atmosphere.

🔁 D6 ✉ 80 West Bow EH1 2HH ☎ 0131 226 7667 🚌 23, 27, 41

CABARET VOLTAIRE

www.thecabaretvoltaire.com
Housed in old subterranean vaults in the Cowgate district, this club is a twin-roomed venue hosting some great gigs. You'll find all types of music, with some 30 live acts a month.

🔁 E6 ✉ 36 Blair Street EH1 1QR ☎ 0131 247 4704 🚌 5, 7, 14, 29, 35, 37 ⏰ Nightly (check for times)

CAMEO

www.picturehouses.co.uk
Cameo, one of the oldest cinemas in Scotland still in use, is a small, comfortable cinema showing low-key Hollywood, international and independent films.

🔁 B8 ✉ 38 Home Street EH3 9LZ ☎ 0871 704 2052 (booking line); 0871 902 5723 🚌 10, 11, 15, 16, 17, 23, 27, 37

EDINBURGH FESTIVAL THEATRE

www.edtheatres.com
This theater, with its distinctive glass facade, has one of the largest stages in Europe. It hosts a range of international dance productions, plays, variety and comedy, from contemporary ballet to performances from the Scottish Opera.

🔁 F7 ✉ 13–29 Nicolson Street EH8 9FT ☎ 0131 529 6000 🚌 2, 3, 5, 7, 8, 14, 29, 31, 33, 37, 42, 49

ESPIONAGE

www.espionage007.co.uk
Dance the night away at this popular complex, with its four spy-themed bars and one dance floor.

🔁 D6 ✉ 9 Victoria Street EH1 1EX ☎ 0131 477 7007 ⏰ Nightly 7pm–3am (to 5am during Festival) 🚌 2, 23, 27, 41

CELTIC MUSIC

Edinburgh pubs and dinner shows are the best places to track down a genuine Celtic music session. Celtic music originates from the seven Celtic regions—Scotland, Ireland, Wales, Isle of Man, Cornwall, Brittany and Galicia. The following city pubs have fine singers and musicians performing on a regular basis: Sandy Bells Bar (✉ Forrest Road EH1 2QH ☎ 0131 225 2751); The Tass (✉ Corner of High Street and St. Mary's Street EH1 1SR ☎ 0131 556 6338, ▷ 64); The Royal Oak (✉ Infirmary Street EH1 1LT ☎ 0131 557 2976). Dates and times can be erratic—check first.

FILMHOUSE

www.filmhousecinema.com
Opposite the Usher Hall, this art-house cinema has three screens that feature the best in art-house and foreign-language cinema from around the globe.

🔁 B7 ✉ 88 Lothian Road EH3 9BZ ☎ 0131 228 2688 🚌 10, 11, 15, 17, 16, 34

FRANKENSTEIN PUB

www.frankensteinedinburgh.co.uk
In a former Pentecostal church, Frankenstein is a bar, restaurant and nightclub themed to bring a chill to the spine. Have a meal, take a drink in one of the three bars or join a themed party, karaoke or games night.

🔁 E7 ✉ 26 George IV Bridge EH1 1EN ☎ 0131 622 1818 ⏰ Daily noon–1am 🚌 23, 27, 41, 42

GREYFRIARS BOBBY

In front of Greyfriars Kirk and named after the famous dog, this wooden-fronted building houses a traditional, friendly pub.

🔁 E7 ✉ 34 Candlemaker Row EH1 2QE ☎ 0131 225 8328 🚌 27, 35, 41, 42

JOLLY JUDGE

www.jollyjudge.co.uk
A delightful little pub with 17th-century character, including a low-beamed ceiling and a wide choice of malt whiskies. It's difficult to find but worth the search.

🔁 D6 ✉ 7 James Court, off Lawnmarket EH1 2PB

☎ 0131 225 2669 🚌 23, 27, 35, 41, 42

KING'S THEATRE
www.edtheatres.com
One of Edinburgh's oldest theaters, housed in a handsome Edwardian building. A diverse range of shows and musicals, pantomime, comedy, plays and international opera are performed during the Festival.
✚ C8 ✉ 2 Leven Street EH3 9LQ ☎ 0131 529 6000 🚌 11, 15, 16, 17, 23

ODEON
www.odeon.co.uk
Centrally located five-screen cinema with the latest sound systems, showing all the big mainstream movies.
✚ B7 ✉ 118 Lothian Road EH3 8BG ☎ 0871 224 4007 🚌 10, 11, 15, 16, 17, 34, 37

QUEEN'S HALL
www.thequeenshall.net
In a converted church, this intimate venue offers a range of events, from jazz and blues to rock and classical music, and comedy from top-class performers. Home to the Scottish Chamber Orchestra.
✚ F9 ✉ 85–89 Clerk Street EH8 9JG ☎ 0131 668 2019 🚌 3, 5, 7, 8, 29, 31, 37

ROYAL LYCEUM THEATRE
www.lyceum.org.uk
A magnificent Victorian theater that creates all its own shows. Con-

temporary and classic productions feature, as well as new works.
✚ B7 ✉ Grindlay Street EH3 9AX ☎ 0131 248 4848 (box office) 🚌 1, 10, 11, 15, 16, 17, 22, 34

THOMSON'S BAR
www.thomsonsbar edinburgh.co.uk
Winner of several real ale and independent beer awards, this refurbished pub has a wonderful interior packed with old adverts and mirrors.

INTERNATIONAL FILM FESTIVAL
Edinburgh International Film Festival is the longest-running event of its kind in the world, having produced innovative and exciting cinema since 1947. It began with a focus on documentary film, and evolved into a pioneering force for the world of cinema. A celebration of cinema and a showcase for new films from all over the world, it presents UK and world premieres, video shorts and animation. The festival takes place across Edinburgh's cinemas and now runs for two weeks in June (it used to be held in August, running concurrently with the Fringe). For information, contact the Edinburgh International Film Festival (✉ 88 Lothian Road EH3 9BZ ☎ 0131 228 4051 or 0131 623 8030; www.edfilmfest.org.uk).

✚ A7 ✉ 182–184 Morrison Street EH3 8EB ☎ 0131 228 5700 🕐 Daily 12–12 🚌 2

TRAVERSE THEATRE
www.traverse.co.uk
State-of-the-art venue next to the Usher Hall, respected for its experimental plays and dance productions; you can see hot new work by Scottish playwrights.
✚ B7 ✉ 10 Cambridge Street EH1 2ED ☎ 0131 228 1404 🚌 10, 11, 22

UNDER THE STAIRS
www.underthestairs.org
This venue is especially popular with Edinburgh's younger trendy crowd. There are plenty of cocktails to choose from, served to you by the experienced staff, and a variety of music to chill out to. Changing pieces of art and photography grace the walls of the chic interior.
✚ E7 ✉ 3A Merchant Street EH1 2QD ☎ 0131 466 8550 🕐 Mon–Sat noon–1am, Sun noon–midnight 🚌 23, 27, 41, 42

USHER HALL
www.usherhall.co.uk
Usher Hall is a prestigious venue that attracts the very best performers. The list has included José Carreras, the English Chamber Orchestra and the Moscow Philharmonic.
✚ B7 ✉ Lothian Road EH1 2EA ☎ 0131 228 1155 🚌 1, 10, 11, 15, 16, 17, 22, 34

Restaurants

PRICES

Prices are approximate, based on a 3-course meal for one person.
£££ over £25
££ £15–£25
£ under £15

AMBER RESTAURANT (££)

www.amber-restaurant.co.uk
In the Scotch Whisky Experience (▷ 31), Amber offers a lunchtime menu of Scottish cuisine for visitors to the attraction and shoppers. The ambience is transformed in the evening, with soft velvet drapes enclosing a more intimate space. It's a romantic setting for a first-class meal, with delights such as hot smoked salmon with whisky-honey mustard mayonnaise followed by tournedos of Scottish beef fillet wrapped in pancetta.
✚ D6 ✉ 354 Castlehill, The Royal Mile EH1 2NE
☎ 0131 477 8477 ◔ Lunch daily 12–3.45, dinner Tue–Sat from 7 🚌 23, 27, 41, 42

ANGELS WITH BAGPIPES (££)

www.angelswithbagpipes.co.uk
A sophisticated restaurant which stands out from the run-of-the-mill eating places in this part of town and serves imaginative Scottish-fusion dishes. There's a courtyard where you can eat outdoors on sunny days.

✚ E6 ✉ 343 High Street EH1 1PW ☎ 0131 222 1111 ◔ Daily 12–10 🚌 23, 27, 41, 42, 67

BENNETS BAR (£)

Popular with actors from the nearby King's Theatre, this Victorian bar prides itself on sound, simple, homemade food at a good price, and 100 or so malt whiskies. The elaborate interior includes stained glass, tiles, mirrors and carved wood.
✚ B9 ✉ 8 Leven Street EH3 9LG ☎ 0131 229 5143 ◔ Bar meals: Mon–Sat noon–2, 5–8.30 🚌 11, 17, 23

TIPS FOR EATING OUT

Many Edinburgh restaurants can seat customers who walk in off the street, but if you have your heart set on eating at a particular establishment reserve a table in advance. Most restaurants are happy to serve a one- or two-course meal, if that is all you want. If you pay by credit card, when you key in your PIN you may be prompted to leave a tip. It's acceptable to ignore this and leave a cash tip instead. The normal amount, assuming you are happy with the service, is about 10 percent. In Edinburgh it is fairly common for a reservation to last only a couple of hours, after which time you will be expected to vacate the table for the next sitting.

DEACON BRODIE'S TAVERN (£)

This pub is a popular spot for locals and visitors alike, with its traditional atmosphere. Bar snacks downstairs, restaurant upstairs. Find out more about the infamous Brodie, one of the inspirations for Stevenson's Dr. Jekyll and Mr. Hyde, while you sip your pint.
✚ D6 ✉ 435 Lawnmarket EH1 2NT ☎ 0131 225 6531 ◔ Daily, normal pub hours 🚌 23, 27, 35, 41, 42

EDINBURGH LARDER (£)

www.edinburghlarder.co.uk
This café serves cakes, salads, snacks and delicious sandwiches made from the best of Scottish produce, including venison and smoked salmon on artisan breads and rolls. It also serves gourmet teas and coffees, as well as a limited range of wines and beers.
✚ F6 ✉ 15 Blackfriars Street EH1 1NB ☎ 0131 556 6922 ◔ Mon–Sat 8–5, Sun 9–5 🚌 35

ELEPHANT HOUSE (£)

www.elephanthouse.biz
A popular café offering snacks, light meals and a mouthwatering array of cakes, accompanied by excellent coffees and teas.
✚ E6 ✉ 21 George IV Bridge EH1 1EN ☎ 0131 220 5355 ◔ Coffee, lunch, dinner 🚌 23, 27, 41, 42

GRAIN STORE (££–£££)

www.grainstore-restaurant.co.uk

This smart restaurant has a unique setting in an 18th-century stone vaulted storeroom with archways and intimate alcoves. The well-balanced menu includes such delights as roe deer, beetroot parcel and rosemary, using the very best of Scottish produce. Very tempting homemade desserts. Good set-price meals, too.

🔁 D6 ✉ 30 Victoria Street (1st floor) EH1 2JW ☎ 0131 225 7635 🕐 Lunch, dinner 🚍 2, 23, 27, 41

HANAM'S (££)

www.hanams.com

This restaurant has several colorful rooms over two floors, plus an open-air terrace for summer dining. The menu is authentically Kurdish, with dishes such as *gormeh sabzi* (Persian-style lamb in spinach) and lamb *tashreeb*, a rich spicy stew. Hanam's does not have a license, but you can bring your own wine or beers.

🔁 D6 ✉ 3 Johnston Terrace EH1 2PW ☎ 0131 225 1329 🕐 Daily 12–11 🚍 23, 27, 41, 42, 67

THE MITRE (££)

www.nicholsonspubs.co.uk

Part of a chain which also includes the legendary Deacon Brodie's further up the Mile, the Mitre serves decent pub food (steak and ale pie, fish and chips, steak and so on) in an attractive old building. There's a good range of real ales and malt whiskies, too.

🔁 F6 ✉ 133 High Street EH1 1SG ☎ 0131 652 3902 🕐 Mon–Thu 12–12, Fri–Sat noon–1am 🚍 35

MONTEITHS (£££)

www.monteithsrestaurant.co.uk

Monteith's is more sophisticated in every way than most places on this stretch of the Royal Mile. The bar, with its leather armchairs, has a clubby feel, as does the dining room. The menu is reminiscent of a grand Scottish country house, with a good choice of game such as pheasant and wood pigeon in season, as well as meltingly tender pork and perfectly pink lamb.

🔁 F6 ✉ 57–61 High Street EH1 1SR ☎ 0131 557 0330 🕐 Mon–Fri dinner only, Sat–Sun 12–10 🚍 35

MUMS (££)

www.monstermashcafe.co.uk

Sausage and mashed potato is staging a comeback here. The bangers come in many varieties, such as Auld Reekie (smoked) and Mediterranean (with basil and sun-dried tomatoes), and there is a variety of mash, too. Plastic tomato-shaped ketchup bottles add a large helping of nostalgia.

🔁 E7 ✉ 4a Forrest Road EH1 2QN ☎ 0131 260 9806 🕐 Breakfast, lunch, dinner 🚍 35, 45

NORTH BRIDGE BRASSERIE (£££)

www.northbridgebrasserie.com

In the five-star boutique hotel The Scotsman, this restaurant uses local produce to fine effect, with the menu including Perthshire lamb or Loch Tarber scallops.

🔁 E6 ✉ The Scotsman Hotel, 20 North Bridge EH1 1YT ☎ 0131 556 5565 🕐 Lunch, dinner 🚍 3, 5, 7, 30, 31, 33, 37

OINK (£)

www.oinkhogroast.co.uk

This popular, no-nonsense café serves great hog rolls, made famous in the Farmers' Market. The hog

---

PUB GRUB

Central-city dining pubs traditionally serve snacks and light meals such as sandwiches, toasted sandwiches, filled potatoes and ploughmans (bread, cheese and pickles). Nowadays, many have extended their menu to include such dishes as curry, steak-and-ale pie, steak and chips or even haggis and neeps (a blend of swede and potato mashed with butter and milk). But, on the whole, pub food in Scotland is not overly imaginative.

roast is displayed prominently in the window. You can have your roll with or without crackling (salted crunchy pork rind), and choose your relish. Find a seat if you can, or take out. There is a second establishment at 82 Canongate.

➕ D6 ✉ 34 Victoria Street EH1 2JW ☎ 07771 968233 🕐 Daily 10am–11pm 🚌 2, 23, 27, 41

ONDINE (£££)

www.ondinerestaurant.co.uk
Seafood tops the bill at this smart restaurant beneath the stylish Missoni Hotel. The roast shellfish platter is a tasty melange of clams, lobster, mussels and langoustines. Other good fish dishes include sea bass and John Dory. Service is attentive, and the overall atmosphere is pleasantly unstuffy.

➕ E7 ✉ 2 George IV Bridge EH1 1AD ☎ 0131 226 1888 🕐 Lunch, dinner 🚌 23, 27, 41, 42, 67

ONE SQUARE (££)

www.onesquareedinburgh.co.uk
This smart new bar-restaurant close to the theater district is handy for dinner or drinks before or after a show. The menu features classic British cooking based on fine Scottish ingredients ranging from Black Isle beef to west coast scallops and oysters, Stornoway black pudding and Shetland mussels.

➕ B7 ✉ 1 Festival Square EH3 9SR ☎ 0131 221 6422 🕐 Daily 8pm–1am 🚌 1, 10, 11, 15, 16, 24, 34, 36, 36, 47

PETIT PARIS (££)

www.petitparis-restaurant.co.uk
France meets Scotland at this friendly country-style bistro. The authentic French cooking features regional specialties—for example from Alsace. The restaurant is a member of Slow Food Scotland.

➕ D7 ✉ 38–40 Grassmarket EH1 2JU ☎ 0131 226 2442 🕐 Daily lunch, dinner; closed Mon Oct–Mar 🚌 2

FOOD ON THE RUN

Edinburgh has lots of quick options when you don't want to stop for long. There are food courts in shopping malls, while many attractions have their own restaurants and cafés. American fast-food chains have reached most corners of Scotland, so you won't have to look far to find a pizza or hamburger. The city is liberally sprinkled with very good take-out sandwich bars. Although Edinburgh has many traditional cafés, the word 'café' is used to describe the increasing number of more stylish Continental-style establishments, which bridge the gap between pubs, restaurants and coffee bars by selling coffees, snacks, wines and meals.

TOWER RESTAURANT (£££)

www.tower-restaurant.com
On the fifth floor of the National Museum of Scotland, with great views of the castle, this chic, stylish restaurant offers an interesting selection of eclectic dishes using quality Scottish ingredients.

➕ E7 ✉ National Museum of Scotland, Chambers Street EH1 1JF ☎ 0131 225 0973 🕐 Lunch, dinner 🚌 2, 23, 27, 35, 41, 42

WHISKI ROOMS (££)

www.whiskirooms.co.uk
This world-class whisky bar and bistro offers a choice of some 300 single malts and blended whiskies. The menu emphasizes Scottish beef, lamb, steaks and seafood and there are some temptingly sticky puddings.

➕ D6 ✉ 4–7 North Bank Street EH1 2HP ☎ 0131 225 7224 🕐 Daily 12–10 🚌 23, 27, 41, 42, 67

WITCHERY BY THE CASTLE (£££)

www.thewitchery.com
This enchanting candlelit restaurant is the place for a special night out. The cooking adds a contemporary twist to Scottish classics like game, fish and shellfish. There is a huge selection of wines.

➕ D6 ✉ Castlehill, Royal Mile EH1 2NF ☎ 0131 225 5613 🕐 Lunch, dinner 🚌 23, 27, 35, 41, 42

At the east end of the Royal Mile is the Canongate, culminating in the modern Scottish Parliament Building, the Palace of Holyroodhouse and the open space of Holyrood Park to relax in after sightseeing.

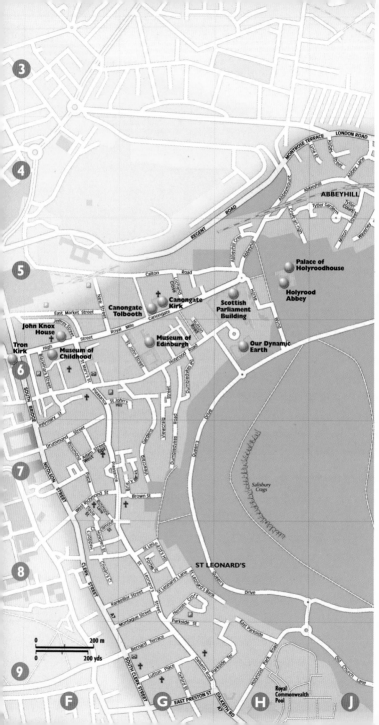

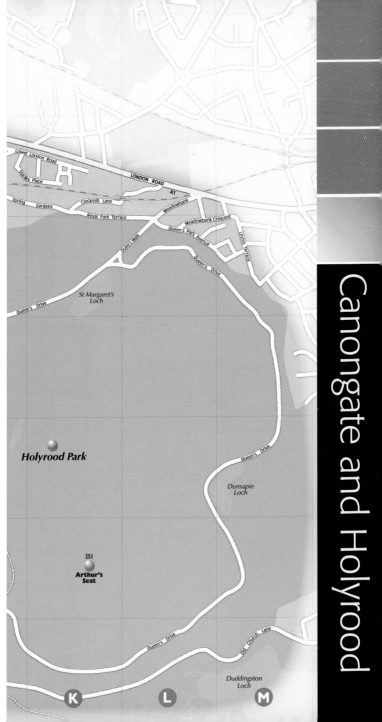

Arthur's Seat

HIGHLIGHTS

● Spectacular views
● The walk to the top
● Dunsapie Loch and bird reserve

TIP

● Try to pick a clear day to get the best from the views. It's a waste to make the effort if it's a "dreich" day, as the Scots call a dismal day.

The perfect antidote to the stresses of the city, with spectacular views, Arthur's Seat is the remains of an extinct volcano 325 million years old, and it's right on Edinburgh's doorstep.

Geological background The green hill of Arthur's Seat is a city landmark, 251m (823ft) high and visible for miles. Formed during the early Carboniferous era, it is surrounded by seven smaller hills. The summit marks where the cone erupted and molten rock from the volcano formed the high cliffs of Salisbury Crags. During the Ice Age, erosion exposed the twin peaks of Arthur's Seat and the Crow Hill. There are a variety of explanations for the name; some say it is a corruption of the Gaelic name for archers, others that the Normans associated it with King Arthur.

Clockwise from top left: view of Salisbury Crags from the foot of Arthur's Seat; for a great view over the city it is worth the climb up to Arthur's Seat; scaling the heights; silhouette of Salisbury Crags at dusk; Arthur's Seat overlooking Edinburgh, as seen from the city's Royal Observatory on Blackford Hill

Get active There is open access to Arthur's Seat, the hills and four small lochs, all of which are part of the Royal Park of Holyrood. It is worth the climb to the top for the views over the Palace of Holyroodhouse and beyond. Start your climb from a path near St. Margaret's Well, just inside the palace's entrance to the park. The path divides at the start of Hunter's Bog valley but both branches lead to the summit. The right-hand path will take you along the Radical Road that runs beneath the rock face of the Salisbury Crags. The left path goes through Piper's Walk to the top. You'll find parking at the palace, in Duddingston village and by the pools of St. Margaret's Loch and Dunsapie Loch, which has a bird reserve. From the loch it is just a short climb over some rocks to the top. From here the whole panorama of Edinburgh, plus the Firth of Forth, the Pentland hills and the coast, is below.

THE BASICS

✚ K7–8
✉ Holyrood Park
🕐 24 hours, 365 days, but no vehicular access to the park (except for Dunsapie Loch) on Sun
🚌 35 and then walk through park; or 4, 5, 44, 45 to Meadowbank and walk
🚉 Edinburgh Waverley
♿ Few

Canongate Tolbooth

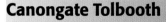

THE PEOPLE

Dating from 1591, this French-style Tolbooth has served as both a council chamber and a prison. It now houses the People's Story, a museum of everyday life since the 18th century.

From toll-house to museum The Tolbooth is the oldest remaining building in this district and marked the boundary between Holyrood and Edinburgh proper. It served as the council chamber for the independent burgh of Canongate until its incorporation into the city in 1856. A five-floor building with a turreted steeple, it was also used as a prison for the burgh. The huge boxed clock that projects above the street was added in 1884.

Edinburgh life The building is now home to the People's Story, a museum dedicated to everyday

Clockwise from far left: the turreted Canongate Tolbooth, home to the People's Story museum; trade union banners; passing the time down the pub, one of the museum's displays; the struggle for the right to vote, the people of Edinburgh on the march; all aboard—a clippie model at the museum; the museum sign

life and times in Edinburgh from the 18th century up to the present day. Using oral history, written sources and the reminiscences of local people, it creates a fascinating insight. Indulge your senses through the visual displays, sounds and smells that evoke life in a prison cell, a draper's shop and a cooper's (barrel maker's) workshop. See a servant at work and a tramcar conductor (a clippie, who clipped the tickets). The museum portrays the struggle for improved conditions, better health and ways to enjoy what little leisure the citizens had. The trades union movement and friendly societies played a big part in the struggle for people's rights and they feature in the museum.

Time off Check out the places the locals went to for gossip, such as the re-created pub, the tearoom and the washhouse.

THE BASICS

www.edinburghmuseums.
org.uk
✚ G5
✉ 163 Canongate
EH8 8BN
☎ 0131 529 4057
🕐 Mon–Sat 10–5; also
Sun 12–5 in Aug
🚌 35
🚉 Edinburgh Waverley
♿ Good
💷 Free
❓ Shop stocks a wide
range of local social
history books

Holyrood Park

TOP 25

Arthur's Seat, at the heart of Holyrood Park (left); festival time in the park (right)

THE BASICS

www.historic-scotland.gov.uk

➕ K7

✉ Holyrood Park

☎ Historic Scotland Ranger Service: 0131 652 8150

🕐 24 hours, 365 days a year, but no vehicular access to the park (except for Dunsapie Loch) on Sun

🚌 35 to palace entrance; other buses to perimeter

🚆 Edinburgh Waverley

♿ Varies, phone for details

🎟 Free

❓ Leaflets with walking routes are available from staff in the hut in Broad Street car park (by Holyrood Palace) and from the Holyrood Lodge Information Centre (by the Scottish Parliament), daily 9.30–3.30

HIGHLIGHTS

● Arthur's Seat (▷ 48–49)
● Dunsapie Loch
● St. Margaret's Well

It's unusual—and a pleasant surprise—to discover a city park containing such wild countryside. You'll even find small lochs within Edinburgh's Holyrood Park.

City's green treasure A royal park since the 12th century, Holyrood Park was enclosed by a stone boundary wall in 1541. Spreading out behind the Palace of Holyroodhouse (▷ 58–59), it extends to some 263ha (650 acres) and is dominated by the great extinct volcano Arthur's Seat (▷ 48–49). It represents a microcosm of Scottish landscape, boasting four lochs, open moorland, marshes, glens and dramatic cliffs, the Salisbury Crags, which inspired Sir Arthur Conan Doyle's novel *The Lost World*.

Get your boots on The park is circled by Queen's Drive, built at the instigation of Prince Albert and closed to commercial vehicles. The area around Dunsapie Loch gives a real sense of remote countryside and is a good spot to start the ascent to Arthur's Seat. It is particularly peaceful here when cars are prohibited on Sunday. Altogether, Holyrood Park is an excellent place to walk, cycle or picnic.

More to see Also in the park is St. Margaret's Well, a medieval Gothic structure near the palace, where a clear spring wells from beneath sculpted vaulting. Above St. Margaret's Loch, a 19th-century artificial lake, are the remains of St. Anthony's Chapel. On the edge of the park you will find Duddingston village, with one of the oldest pubs in Edinburgh, and the attractive Duddingston Loch.

Museum of Edinburgh

The home of Edinburgh's own museum is Huntly House, a 16th-century dwelling much altered in subsequent centuries and at one time occupied by a trade guild.

Picturesque house Just across the road from the Canongate Tolbooth and the People's Story (▷ 50–51), the building housing the Museum of Edinburgh is distinguished by its three pointed gables. Robert Chambers, a Victorian antiquarian, called Huntly House "the speaking house" owing to the Latin inscriptions on the facade.

What's on show Inside the museum is a treasure house of local details that brings the history of the city to life. The collections include maps and prints, silver, glass and a vibrant assortment of old shop signs. There is also a fine collection of Edinburgh ceramics and examples of Scottish pottery, as well as items relating to Field Marshal Earl Haig, commander of the British Expeditionary Force in World War I. Of particular interest is the collar and bowl that once belonged to Greyfriars Bobby (▷ 26), together with the original plaster model for the bronze statue of the dog in Candlemaker Row. The museum regularly presents temporary exhibitions that further highlight aspects of local life and are drawn from the extensive local history and decorative arts collections.

Historical Covenant Also on show is the original National Covenant signed by Scotland's Presbyterian leadership in 1638, which is one of the city's greatest treasures.

THE BASICS

www.edinburghmuseums.org.uk

➕ G6

✉ Huntly House, 142 Canongate, Royal Mile EH8 8DD

☎ 0131 529 4143

🕐 Mon–Sat 10–5; also Sun 12–5 during Aug

🚌 35

🚉 Edinburgh Waverley

♿ Poor

🎟 Free

HIGHLIGHTS

- Huntly House building
- Greyfriars Bobby—collar and bowl
- National Covenant
- Earl Haig memorabilia

Museum of Childhood

HIGHLIGHTS

● Extensive toy collection
● Re-creation of 1930s classroom
● Victorian dolls
● Dolls' houses
● Automata

TIP

● Check in advance for the schedule of regularly changing exhibitions and varied events to get the most out of your visit.

This has been described as "the noisiest museum in the world" and it is popular with both children and adults. Introduce your children to the past and maybe relive it yourself.

Nostalgic pleasure The Museum of Childhood is a delight and claims to be the first museum in the world dedicated to the history of childhood. It was the brainchild of town councillor Joseph Patrick Murray, who argued that the museum was about children rather than for them. Opened in 1955, the collection has grown to display a nostalgic treasure trove of dolls and dolls' houses, train sets and teddy bears. Every aspect of childhood is covered here, from education and medicine to clothing and food. Don't miss the re-created 1930s schoolroom, complete with the

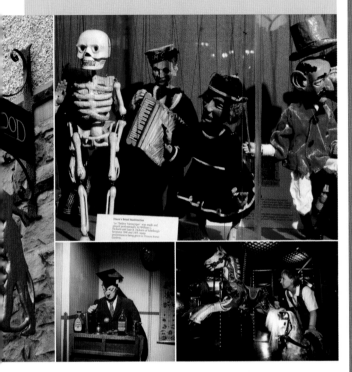

chanting of multiplication tables, and watch the street games of Edinburgh children in the 1950s.

Awakening memories Adults who have never really grown up may well find nostalgic memories of the past. There is a collection of older material such as Victorian dolls and German automata, but probably the best part is recognizing the objects from your own childhood, such as Meccano. If you have children, then a visit will be enjoyable, but even without children, this museum should still be on the "must-visit" list.

Founding father Joseph Patrick Murray said that his museum explored a specialized field of social history. From the early days of the museum he put his own mark on the huge array of exhibits, with his slant on informative labels.

THE BASICS

www.edinburghmuseums. org.uk

⊞ F6

✉ 42 High Street, Royal Mile EH1 1TG

☎ 0131 529 4142

🕐 Mon–Sat 10–5, Sun 12–5

🚌 35 and all North Bridge buses

🚉 Edinburgh Waverley

♿ Very good

🎫 Free

Our Dynamic Earth

In the jaws of a saber-toothed tiger (left); the Restless Earth exhibition (right)

THE BASICS

www.dynamicearth.co.uk

H6

112 Holyrood Road EH8 8AS

0131 550 7800

Apr–Oct daily 10–5.30, (Jul, Aug 10–6); Nov–Mar Wed–Sun 10–5.30

The Food Chain café

35

Edinburgh Waverley

Excellent

Expensive

Well-stocked gift shop—Natural Selection

HIGHLIGHTS

● Striking building
● Time Machine
● Casualties and Survivors gallery
● Tropical Rainforest
● "Submarine trip"
● Restless Earth experience
● FutureDome
● Earthscape Scotland

This tented, spiky roof rising like a white armadillo on the edge of Holyrood Park is Edinburgh's Millennium project: a science park that thrills at every turn.

Popular science This interactive spectacular tells the story of the Earth and its changing nature, from the so-called Big Bang (as viewed from the bridge of a space ship in the How It All Started gallery) to the present day (exactly who lives where in the rain forest).

Stunning effects With 12 galleries devoted to the planet, the underlying message is that the world is a fascinating and ever-changing place. Experience the effect of erupting volcanoes, the icy chill of the polar regions and even a simulated earthquake while lava apparently boils below. You may get caught in a humid rainstorm in the Tropical Rainforest. Every 15 minutes the sky darkens, lightning flashes, thunder roars and torrential rain descends. You can travel in the Time Machine, where numerous stars are created using lights and mirrors. A multiscreen flight over mountains and glaciers is a dizzying highlight. Earthscape Scotland is a trip through geological time and FutureDome is an exciting interactive journey into the future. Casualties and Survivors follows the evolution and adaption of creatures and plants.

Plenty of stamina Our Dynamic Earth is proving a popular, impressive feat of high-tech ingenuity. Hardly a relaxing experience, it's well worth a visit, although peak times are likely to be crowded.

Controversial, expensive but never boring, the extraordinary Scottish Parliament Building

Scottish Parliament Building

With the passing of the Scotland Act in 1998, the first Scottish Parliament since 1707 was established. It has been at this controversial building since 2004.

Setting the scene From 1999, the Scottish Parliament was housed in buildings around the Royal Mile. Debating took place in the Church of Scotland Assembly at the top of the Mound. The then First Minister Donald Dewar commissioned a new parliament building to be constructed opposite Holyrood Palace. At an original estimated cost of around £40 million, the building was finally opened by the Queen in October 2004, by which time the cost had soared to over £400 million. This expense caused a good deal of controversy, but the resulting building has also attracted much praise.

No expense spared Hailed by architects and critics as one of the most significant new buildings in Britain, the complex was the work of Barcelona-based architect Enric Miralles. It is a unique Catalan-Scottish blend. The building is set within landscaped public gardens near the Palace of Holyroodhouse, against a backdrop of the Salisbury Crags. Natural materials have been carefully crafted to a high level of excellence, with expert use of wood, stone and glass. Intricate details in oak and sycamore have been used throughout to offset the granite and smooth concrete finishes. The Debating Chamber, where the 129 members meet, has a striking oak-beamed ceiling. Miralles' expertise combined design with practicality through acute attention to detail.

THE BASICS

www.scottish.parliament.uk

🔢 H5

✉ The Scottish Parliament, Holyrood Road EH99 1SP

☎ 0131 348 5200

🕐 Business days (Tue–Thu) 9–6.30. Non-business days (Mon, Fri–Sat) and when Parliament is in recess Apr–Sep 10–5 (Tue–Thu 9–6.30); Oct–Mar 10–4

🍴 Café 🚻 35

🚉 Edinburgh Waverley

♿ Excellent

🎫 Free; tours moderate

❓ Guided tours lasting 1 hour are available on most non-business days. Reserve tickets for Public Gallery in advance. Shop sells exclusive items branded to the Scottish Parliament

HIGHLIGHTS

● Architecture
● Exhibition on Scottish Parliament
● Public Gallery

Palace of Holyroodhouse

HIGHLIGHTS

- State apartments
- Queen's Gallery
- Chambers of Mary, Queen of Scots

TIP

● It is best to phone ahead as the palace is closed to visitors whenever a member of the royal family is in residence and security surrounding the building is extremely tight.

Founded as a monastery in 1128, today the palace is the Queen's official residence in Scotland. The pepperpot-towered castle is set against the backdrop of majestic Arthur's Seat, at the foot of the Royal Mile.

Steeped in royal history In the 15th century the palace became a guest house for the nearby Holyrood Abbey (now a scenic ruin), and its name is said to derive from the Holy Rood, a fragment of Christ's Cross belonging to King David I (c. 1080–1153). Mary, Queen of Scots stayed here, and a brass plate marks where her Italian favorite, David Rizzio, was murdered in her private apartments in the west tower in 1566. During the Civil War in 1650 the palace was seriously damaged by fire and major

Clockwise from far left: crowning glory—a royal lantern outside the Palace of Holyroodhouse; a stone unicorn stands guard; the mellow evening light enhances the fairy-tale palace; lion detail on the gates; a view of the palace and Arthur's Seat from Calton Hill

rebuilding was necessary. Bonnie Prince Charlie held court here in 1745, followed by George IV on his triumphant visit to the city in 1822, and later by Queen Victoria en route to Balmoral.

Home and art gallery The palace offers all the advantages of exploring a living space steeped in history and filled with works of art from the Royal Collection. More precious artworks are on view in the stunning Queen's Gallery, by the entrance and opposite the new Scottish Parliament. The state rooms, designed by architect William Bruce (1630–1710) for Charles II and hung with Brussels tapestries, are particularly elaborate and ornately splendid. Don't miss the 110 preposterous royal portraits painted in a hurry by Jacob de Wet in 1684–86, which are hung in the Great Gallery.

THE BASICS

www.royalcollection.org.uk
✛ H5
✉ Canongate, Royal Mile EH8 8DX
☎ 0131 556 5100
🕐 Apr–Oct daily 9.30–6; Nov–Mar daily 9.30–4.30. May close at short notice
🍴 In old coach house
🚌 35, 36
🚆 Edinburgh Waverley
♿ Good 💷 Expensive
❓ Free audio tour available. Gift shop stocks cards, books and china

More to See

CANONGATE KIRK

www.canongatekirk.org.uk
Built in 1688, this church's distinctive
Dutch gable and plain interior reflect
the Canongate's trading links with the
Low Countries. Note the gilded stag's
head at the gable top, traditionally
a gift of the monarch. Buried in the
graveyard are the economist and
philosopher Adam Smith (1723–90)
and David Rizzio, darling of Mary,
Queen of Scots, murdered in 1566.
➕ G5 ✉ Canongate EH8 8BR ☎ 0131
556 3515 🕐 Jun–Sep Mon–Sat 10.30–4,
Sun service at 11.15; burial ground open
all year 🚌 35 🚉 Edinburgh Waverley
♿ Good 💷 Free (donations welcomed)

HOLYROOD ABBEY

You can see the abbey ruins only on
a visit to the Palace of Holyroodhouse
(▷ 58–59). The present structure
was built in the early 13th century.
➕ H5 ✉ The Palace of Holyroodhouse
EH8 8DX ☎ 0131 556 5100 🕐 Apr–Oct
daily 9.30–6; Nov–Mar 9.30–4.30. May close at
short notice 🚌 35 🚉 Edinburgh Waverley
♿ Good 💷 Expensive

JOHN KNOX HOUSE

www.tracscotland.org
Dating to the 15th century, the house
is typical of the period, with over-
hanging gables and picturesque win-
dows. Inside is a museum with dis-
plays relating to Knox and to James
Mosman, jeweler to Mary, Queen of
Scots. The house is also home to the
Scottish Storytelling Centre (▷ 64).
➕ F6 ✉ 43–45 High Street EH1 1SR
☎ 0131 556 9579 🕐 Mon–Sat 10–6, Sun
(Jul, Aug only) 12–6 🚌 35 and all North
Bridge buses 🚉 Edinburgh Waverley
♿ Ground floor only 💷 Moderate

TRON KIRK

This fine early Scottish Renaissance
church was built between 1637 and
1663. Its name derives from the salt-
tron, a public weighbeam that once
stood outside. The church has not
been a place of worship since 1952,
and is now open in July and August
as a concert venue and hub of the
Edinburgh Jazz Festival.
➕ E6 ✉ High Street EH1 2NG 🚌 35 and all
North Bridge buses 🚉 Edinburgh Waverley

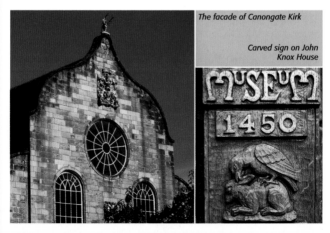

The facade of Canongate Kirk

Carved sign on John Knox House

Through Canongate to Holyrood Park

Walk along High Street to Canongate, with its historic buildings and museums, and then take a break in the glorious Holyrood Park.

DISTANCE: 1.5km (1 mile) **ALLOW:** 1 hour (plus time in the park)

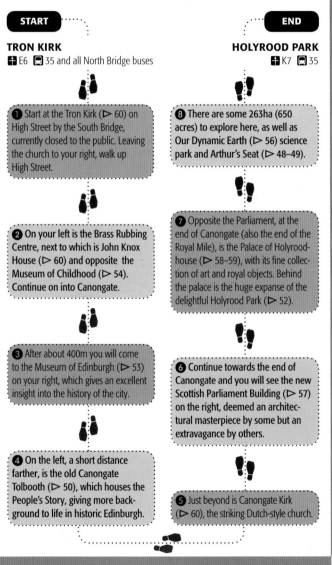

START

TRON KIRK
⊞ E6 🚌 35 and all North Bridge buses

END

HOLYROOD PARK
⊞ K7 🚌 35

❶ Start at the Tron Kirk (▷ 60) on High Street by the South Bridge, currently closed to the public. Leaving the church to your right, walk up High Street.

❷ On your left is the Brass Rubbing Centre, next to which is John Knox House (▷ 60) and opposite the Museum of Childhood (▷ 54). Continue on into Canongate.

❸ After about 400m you will come to the Museum of Edinburgh (▷ 53) on your right, which gives an excellent insight into the history of the city.

❹ On the left, a short distance farther, is the old Canongate Tolbooth (▷ 50), which houses the People's Story, giving more background to life in historic Edinburgh.

❽ There are some 263ha (650 acres) to explore here, as well as Our Dynamic Earth (▷ 56) science park and Arthur's Seat (▷ 48–49).

❼ Opposite the Parliament, at the end of Canongate (also the end of the Royal Mile), is the Palace of Holyroodhouse (▷ 58–59), with its fine collection of art and royal objects. Behind the palace is the huge expanse of the delightful Holyrood Park (▷ 52).

❻ Continue towards the end of Canongate and you will see the new Scottish Parliament Building (▷ 57) on the right, deemed an architectural masterpiece by some but an extravagance by others.

❺ Just beyond is Canongate Kirk (▷ 60), the striking Dutch-style church.

Shopping

CARSON CLARK
www.carsonclarkgallery.co.uk
This wonderful gallery specializes in antique maps and sea charts from all over the globe, dating from the 16th to 19th centuries, plus reproduction prints.
✚ F6 ✉ 17–21 St. Mary's Street EH1 1TA ☎ 0131 556 4710 🚌 35

FUDGE KITCHEN
www.fudgekitchen.co.uk
This shop positively oozes with 20 different varieties of delectable fudge. All handcrafted using traditional methods and the finest ingredients from a recipe dating from 1830.
✚ F6 ✉ 30 High Street EH1 1TB ☎ 0131 558 1517 🚌 35 and all North Bridge buses

GAMES WORKSHOP
www.games-workshop.com
In the age of computerized gaming, this shop is a time-trip back to the pre-digital heyday of role-playing games. It has been pleasing fanboys with its miniature orcs, dragons, wizards and space marines for more than 25 years and will delight kids and nostalgic parents.
✚ E6 ✉ 136 High Street EH1 1QS ☎ 0131 220 6540 🚌 35 and all North Bridge buses

GEOFFREY (TAILOR) KILTMAKERS
www.geoffreykilts.co.uk
Specialists in traditional, casual and modern kilt-making, and outfitters for men, women and children.
✚ F6 ✉ 57–59 High Street EH1 1SR ☎ 0131 557 0256 🚌 35 and all North Bridge buses

PALENQUE
www.palenquejewellery.co.uk
Palenque specializes in competitively priced, high-quality contemporary silver rings, necklaces, pendants and bracelets and hand-crafted accessories.
✚ F6 ✉ 56 High Street EH1 1TB ☎ 0131 557 9553 🚌 35 and all North Bridge buses

RAGAMUFFIN
www.ragamuffingloves.blogspot.co.uk
Displays of vivid handmade chunky knitwear, scarves, accessories and toys catch your eye in the huge windows of this stylish boutique on the corner of St. Mary's Street.
✚ F6 ✉ 278 Canongate EH8 8AA ☎ 0131 557 6007 🚌 35

BAGPIPES
The bagpipes are synonymous with Scotland. You see them everywhere, from the Military Tattoo in Edinburgh to school sports days and agricultural shows. There are many types, played in a variety of countries throughout the world, and, surprisingly, the bagpipes' origins are not Scottish but possibly ancient Egyptian or Greek.

ROYAL MILE ARMOURIES
www.heritageofscotland.com
With its replica broadswords, daggers, battleaxes, helmets and armor, this shop will bring out your inner barbarian and delight fans of *Braveheart*, *Game of Thrones* and *The Lord of the Rings*.
✚ D6 ✉ 555 Castle Hill EH1 2ND ☎ 0131 225 8580 🚌 23, 27, 41, 42, 67

THE TAPPIT HEN
This tiny shop specializes in traditional Celtic knotwork wedding rings, handmade in precious metals, plus a range of gifts made from pewter.
✚ F6 ✉ 89 High Street EH1 1SG ☎ 0131 557 1852 🚌 35 and all North Bridge buses

WILLIAM CADENHEAD
www.wmcadenhead.com
A quaint shop hidden at the bottom of the Royal Mile, specializing in malt whiskies and old oak-matured Demerara rum.
✚ G6 ✉ 172 Canongate EH8 8BN ☎ 0131 556 5864 🚌 35

YE OLDE CHRISTMAS SHOPPE
www.scottishchristmas.com
This family-run shop sets a festive scene with its Christmassy red facade, warm atmosphere and hand-crafted festive gifts.
✚ G6 ✉ 145 Canongate EH8 8BN ☎ 0131 557 9220 🚌 35

Entertainment and Nightlife

BONGO CLUB
www.thebongoclub.co.uk
By day an arts center, café and exhibition space, Bongo transforms at night into a venue for live music, drama and the club scene.
➕ E7 ✉ 66 Cowgate EH1 1JX ☎ 0131 558 8844
🕐 Daily 10pm–3am (but times can vary) 🚌 35 and all South Bridge buses

THE JAZZ BAR
Edinburgh's leading jazz venue also hosts funk, soul, blues and roots performers from all over the world, with several performances nightly and on afternoons at weekends.

➕ E7 ✉ 1A Chambers Street EH1 1HR ☎ 0131 220 4298 🕐 Mon–Fri 5pm–3am, Sat–Sun 2.30pm–3am; bar open until 5am Jul–Aug
🚌 35, 45 💷 Small door charge (cash only) for most performances; some free gigs

SCOTTISH STORY-TELLING CENTRE
www.tracscotland.org
Refurbished to provide more capacity for its Scottish and children's plays, and story and poetry readings.
➕ F6 ✉ 43–45 High Street EH1 1SR ☎ 0131 556 9579 🕐 Mon–Sat 10–6, Sun (Jul, Aug only) 12–6 🚌 35 and all

North Bridge buses 🦽 Good 💷 Some events are free, some have a charge

WAVERLEY BAR
The walls and ceiling of this tiny, quirky, old-fashioned bar are plastered with posters from long-forgotten bands and Fringe performances from as long ago as the 1950s. It still hosts live music and (on the last Friday of each month) storytelling events.
➕ F6 ✉ 1 St. Mary's Street EH1 1TA ☎ 0131 557 1050
🕐 Daily 7pm–11pm (sometimes later during Festival)
🚌 35 💷 Free

Restaurants

PRICES
Prices are approximate, based on a 3-course meal for one person.
£££ over £25
££ £15–£25
£ under £15

THE CANON'S GAIT (££)
www.canonsgait.com
This lively gastropub offers a good selection of Scottish real ales and an imaginative menu, which features meaty dishes such as sausage and mash or pig's cheek and pig's ear.

➕ G6 ✉ 232 Canongate EH8 8DQ ☎ 0131 556 4481
🕐 Meals Mon–Sat 12–8; bar Mon–Thu 12–11, Fri–Sat noon–1am 🚌 35

VEGETARIAN
David Bann ensures quality and attention to detail at his well-designed bar/restaurant. Natural wood and soft lighting set the mood for modern vegan and vegetarian cuisine. Vegetarianism has never been so cool.
✉ F6 ✉ 56–58 St. Mary's Street EH1 1SX ☎ 0131 556 5888; www.davidbann.co.uk
🕐 Daily from 11am

DUBH PRAIS RESTAURANT (££)
www.dubhpraisrestaurant.com
Truly Scottish fare with the very best haggis, beef, lamb, venison and mouthwatering salmon.
➕ F6 ✉ 123b High Street EH1 1SG ☎ 0131 557 5732
🕐 Dinner Tue–Sat 🚌 23, 27, 35, 41, 42, 45

PANCHO VILLAS (££)
www.panchovillas.co.uk
Fresh, authentic Mexican dishes with a modern twist.
➕ F6 ✉ 240 Canongate EH9 8AB ☎ 0131 557 4416
🕐 Lunch, dinner; closed lunch Sun 🚌 35

The New Town displays Edinburgh's elegant face. The broad Georgian streets are lined with gracious houses with large windows and attractive doorways. Here, too, are the best shopping and eating opportunities.

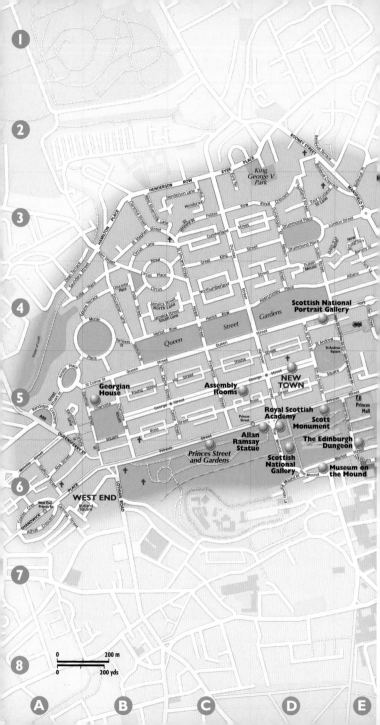

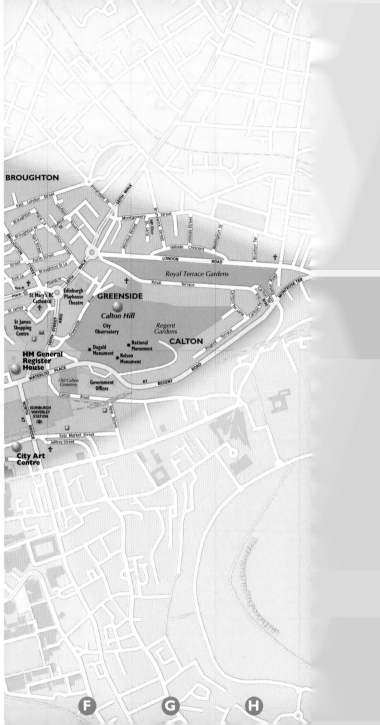

Calton Hill

TOP 25

Edinburgh or Athens? The remarkable Classical buildings of Calton Hill

THE BASICS

www.edinburghmuseums.org.uk

F4

X26

Edinburgh Waverley

Edinburgh Museums and Galleries

0131 556 2716

HIGHLIGHTS

- Spectacular views
- Nelson Monument
- National Monument
- City Observatory
- Playfair Monument
- Dugald Steward Monument

Remarkable buildings grace the top of this volcanic hill, and it is also worth the climb for superb views over the city—Robert Louis Stevenson's most-loved vista of Edinburgh.

Grandiose style Calton Hill (108m/354ft) is crowned by the columns of one of Edinburgh's more eccentric edifices. In 1822 work began on the National Monument of Scotland. Inspired by the Parthenon in Athens and built by public subscription, it was to be a monument to Scottish sailors and soldiers killed in the Napoleonic Wars, but in 1829—with only 12 columns completed—the money ran out. The prolific Edinburgh architect William Playfair's grandiose monument became known as "Edinburgh's Disgrace." The remaining folly, however, is part of the distinctive skyline of Calton Hill.

Other monuments Sharing the slopes of Calton Hill with the National Monument are the City Observatory (designed by James Craig) and the Dugald Steward Monument, another design by William Playfair. Also on the hill is the 1816 tower of the Nelson Monument, a 143-step climb, but worth the effort. The climb to the park at the top is rewarded by superb views. Here on the grassy slopes you can see south to the red-toned cliffs of Salisbury Crags and down to the undulating slopes of Holyrood Park or to the east beyond Princes Street. Despite its grand Classical structures, Calton Hill is still very much revered as common ground to many locals.

Robert Adam's
Georgian House (right)
has some classic 18th-
century displays (left)

TOP
25

Georgian House

This elegant house, with its preserved period interiors, gives you the chance to glimpse into the lives of the prosperous classes who lived in the New Town in the 18th century.

How the other half lived The north side of Charlotte Square is the epitome of 18th-century New Town elegance and was designed by architect Robert Adam (1728–92) as a single, palace-fronted block. With its symmetrical stone-work, rusticated base and ornamented upper levels, it is an outstanding example of the style. The Georgian House, a preserved residence on the north side of the square, oozes gracious living. It is a meticulous re-creation by the National Trust for Scotland, reflecting all the fashionable details of the day, right down to the Wedgwood dinner service on the dining table and the magnificent drawing room with its beautiful candlesticks.

Georgian elegance The 18th-century monied classes knew what they wanted. As you step in the door of this house you can't help but be impressed by the balustraded staircase and its stunning cupola above, flooding the building with light. The stairs lead to the first floor and the Grand Drawing Room, perfect for entertaining.

Below stairs For a contrast, take a look in the basement at the kitchen and the well-scrubbed areas, including the wine cellar and china closet. Here the hard work took place, reflecting the marked social divides of the time.

THE BASICS

www.nts.org.uk
+ B5
⊠ 7 Charlotte Square
EH2 4DR
☎ 0844 493 2118
🕐 Mar daily 10–4; Apr–
Jun, Sep, Oct 10–5;
Jul, Aug 10–6; Nov 11–3
🚌 10, 19, 33, 41 and tram
🚉 Edinburgh Waverley
♿ Limited; six steps to
ground floor
💷 Moderate

HIGHLIGHTS

- Staircase and cupola
- Grand Drawing Room
- Dining Room
- Basement with kitchen

Scottish National Gallery

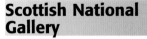

HIGHLIGHTS

● *The Revd Dr Robert Walker Skating on Duddingston Loch* by Sir Henry Raeburn
● Monet's *Haystacks*
● Botticelli's *The Virgin Adoring the Sleeping Christ Child*
● Land- and seascapes by William McTaggart
● Works by Old Masters, including Vermeer, Raphael and Titian

This striking mid-19th-century Classical revival building houses superb Old Masters and an outstanding Scottish collection. It is the perfect setting for Scotland's finest art.

Artistic venue The gallery was designed by New Town architect William Playfair (1789–1857) and completed in the year of his death. It is easily spotted thanks to the huge golden stone pillars of its neoclassical flanks and should not be confused with the nearby Royal Scottish Academy, which has been refurbished as an international exhibition venue (▷ 76).

What's on show The gallery's impressive collection of paintings, sculptures and drawings includes more than 20,000 items, displayed in

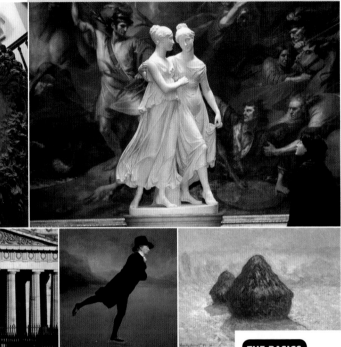

Clockwise from far left: Botticelli's *Virgin Adoring the Sleeping Christ Child, c1490*; busts adorn the gallery stairs; the pretty sculpture is in direct contrast to Benjamin West's *Fury of the Stag, 1786*; Monet's *Haystacks: Snow Effect, 1891*; Raeburn's *The Revd Dr Robert Walker Skating, c.1795*; the grandiose facade of the gallery

intimate and accessible surroundings. The time span runs from the early Renaissance to the end of the 19th century. At the collection's heart are paintings by the great masters of Europe, including Vermeer, Van Gogh, Raphael and Titian. Look out for Monet's *Haystacks* (1891), Velázquez's *Old Woman Cooking Eggs* (1618) and Botticelli's masterpiece *Virgin Adoring the Sleeping Christ Child* (*c.*1490).

Scottish contingent Not surprisingly, the gallery has an outstanding collection of works by Scottish artists. Preferences here include Raeburn's 1795 portrait of *The Revd Dr Robert Walker Skating,* and the sweeping land- and seascapes of William McTaggart. Look out for the vivid scenes of every-day life among the common people, as captured on canvas by Sir David Wilkie.

THE BASICS

www.nationalgalleries.org
⊞ D6
✉ The Mound EH2 2EL
☎ 0131 624 6200
🕐 Daily 10–5, Thu until 7pm
🍴 Café
🚌 3, 10, 17, 23, 24, 27, 44 and others, and tram; a free bus links the National Gallery with the Gallery of Modern Art
🚆 Edinburgh Waverley
♿ Very good
🎫 Free
❓ Shop stocks cards, books and gifts

New Town

HIGHLIGHTS

- Charlotte Square
- The Georgian House
  (▷ 69)
- The Mound

A product of the lack of space in Edinburgh's Old Town, this spectacular piece of Georgian town planning was instigated by a competition in 1766 to build a fine "New Town".

Georgian streets Edinburgh's so-called New Town covers an area of about 318ha (1sq mile) to the north of Princes Street, and is characterized by broad streets of spacious terraced houses with large windows and ornamental door arches. The original area comprised three residential boulevards to run parallel with the Old Town ridge: Princes Street, George Street and Queen Street. With a square at each end (St. Andrew and Charlotte), they were also linked by smaller roads—Rose Street and Thistle Street—to shops and other commercial services. While Princes Street has lost its shine

The entrance to this 18th-century house in New Town looks a picture with its floral display (left); created from a huge pile of rubble, the Mound (middle) went on to support Edinburgh's most prestigious art galleries; details of the Georgian ideal, with typical fanlight and porch, and ornate lamp outside (right)

OUND

through commercial activity, wide Charlotte Square, with its preserved Georgian House (▷ 69), is the epitome of the planners' intentions.

Other highlights It took 2 million cartloads of rubble to create the Mound, later home to the National Gallery (▷ 70–71) and the Royal Scottish Academy (▷ 76). The Mound came about by accident, when "Geordie" Boyd, a clothier in the Old Town, started to dump rubble in the marsh. Soon the builders from the New Town joined in as they dug out foundations for the new buildings. Another highlight of New Town is Stockbridge, a former mining village developed as part of the second New Town. It was on land owned by the painter Sir Henry Raeburn and went on to become a Bohemian artisans' corner. Ann Street is now one of the city's most exclusive addresses.

THE BASICS

✚ D5

🛈 Edinburgh and Scotland Information Centre, 3 Princes Street EH2 2QP ☎ 0845 225 5121

🚆 Edinburgh Waverley

Princes Street and Gardens

TOP
25

Edinburgh's most famous street at dusk (left); Ross fountain in the gardens (right)

THE BASICS

➕ C5/C6
✉ Princes Street
🕐 Gardens: 7am–10pm summer, 7–5 winter
🚉 Edinburgh Waverley
♿ Free

HIGHLIGHTS

● Great views to the castle
● Jenners department store —the world's oldest (▷ 79)
● Floral clock
● Summer band concerts

Originally designed as a residential area, the most famous street in Scotland is now where local people come to shop. The gardens are a welcome escape from the urban buzz.

Changes over time If you stroll along Queen Street today, you can see how it echoes Princes Street and gives an insight into James Craig's original residential plan. He designated today's Thistle and Rose streets, lesser byways between the grand thoroughfares, as the living and business place of tradespeople and shopkeepers. The use of the lanes behind Thistle and Rose streets to reach the back doors of the wealthier residents was a clever element in his simple scheme. By the mid-19th century developments began to encroach from east to west. The gracious Georgian buildings began to deteriorate, some replaced by grim, practical edifices in the 20th century.

Getting its name Princes Street was originally to be called St. Giles Street, but King George III objected as it reminded him of the St. Giles district of London, which was notorious for its lowlife. This famous street became Prince's Street after the Prince Regent, assuming its plural form in 1848.

Oasis of green Princes Street Gardens are a pleasant place to sit down and admire the backs of the Old Town tenements across the valley. In summer there are band concerts to enjoy and, an Edinburgh institution since 1902, the floral clock—a flowerbed planted up as a clock.

More to See

ALLAN RAMSAY STATUE

In the West Princes Street Gardens is a statue of the former wig-maker turned poet Allan Ramsay (1684–1758). The statue is by Sir John Steel (1865).

🔂 D5 ✉ West Princes Street Gardens
🚌 3, 10, 17, 24, 27, 34

ASSEMBLY ROOMS

www.assemblyroomsedinburgh.co.uk
Even if you're not attending a concert here, it's worth visiting to admire the elegance of the rooms, which opened in 1787, in particular the fine ballroom and huge music hall.

🔂 C5 ✉ 54 George Street EH2 2LR ☎ 0131 220 4348 ⏰ Check there is no function
🚌 24, 29, 42 🚉 Edinburgh Waverley
♿ Good 💷 Varies for performances

CITY ART CENTRE

www.edinburghmuseums.org.uk
Established in 1980, the gallery is housed in a six-floor former warehouse. It stages changing exhibitions and displays the city's collection of Scottish paintings, including works by the 20th-century Scottish Colourists.

🔂 E6 ✉ 2 Market Street EH1 1DE
☎ 0131 529 3993 ⏰ Mon–Sat 10–5, Sun 12–5 🍴 Café 🚌 3, 3A, 31, 33, 36
🚉 Edinburgh Waverley ♿ Very good
💷 Free; charge for some exhibitions

THE EDINBURGH DUNGEON

www.thedungeons.com
Deep beneath the paving stones of Edinburgh encounter witch-hunters, grave-robbers and murderers. Not for the fainthearted or very young children.

🔂 E6 ✉ 31 Market Street EH1 1QB
☎ 0131 240 1000 ⏰ Mid-Mar to Jun, Sep, Oct daily 10–5; Jul, Aug daily 10–7; Nov to mid-Mar Mon–Fri 11–4, Sat, Sun 10.30–4.30
🚌 All buses to Waverley Station (one-minute walk) 🚉 Edinburgh Waverley ♿ Phone for details 💷 Expensive

HM GENERAL REGISTER HOUSE

www.nas.gov.uk
Register House was originally sited in the castle, then in the Tolbooth. In 1774 a custom-built Register House was built in Princes Street to house the national archives. It is guarded by a famous statue of Wellington.

Georgian grandeur in the Assembly Rooms

➕ E5 ✉ Scottish Record Office, 2 Princes Street EH1 3YT ☎ 0131 535 1314 🕐 Mon–Fri 9–4.30 🚉 Edinburgh Waverley ♿ Good 💷 Free with reader's ticket; proof of identity required

MUSEUM ON THE MOUND
www.museumonthemound.com
Located in the bank's headquarters, this small, unusual museum displays old maps, prints, gold coins, bank notes, forgeries and bullion chests.
➕ D6 ✉ Bank of Scotland Head Office, The Mound, Edinburgh EH1 1YZ ☎ 0131 243 5464 🕐 Tue–Fri 10–5, Sat, Sun 1–5 and Bank Holiday Mon 🚌 23, 27, 41, 42 🚉 Edinburgh Waverley ♿ Good 💷 Free

ROYAL SCOTTISH ACADEMY
www.royalscottishacademy.org
William Playfair's lovely Classical building has been fully restored and is now linked to the National Gallery to create a superb space for displaying art.
➕ D5 ✉ The Mound EH2 2EL ☎ 0131 225 6671 🕐 Mon–Sat 10–5, Sun 12–5 🚌 3, 10, 17, 23, 24, 27, 44; free bus linking main galleries 🚉 Edinburgh

Waverley ♿ Very good 💷 Free; charge for some exhibitions

SCOTT MONUMENT
www.edinburghmuseums.org.uk
Generations have climbed this 61m (200ft) structure since it opened in 1846 to appreciate fine views of the city. The stone figures are characters from Sir Walter Scott's novels.
➕ D5 ✉ East Princes Street Gardens EH2 2EJ ☎ 0131 529 4068 🕐 Apr–Sep daily 10–7; Oct–Mar daily 10–4 (last admission 3.30) 🚉 Edinburgh Waverley 💷 Moderate

SCOTTISH NATIONAL PORTRAIT GALLERY
www.nationalgalleries.org
This gallery tells the history of Scotland through the portraits of the great and the good, the bad, the beautiful and the vain. A host of familiar faces, including, of course, Robert Burns.
➕ D4 ✉ 1 Queen Street EH2 1JD ☎ 0131 624 6200 🕐 Daily 10–5, Thu until 7 🚌 4, 8, 10, 12, 16, 26, 44; a free bus links main galleries 🚉 Edinburgh Waverley ♿ Very good 💷 Free; charge for some exhibitions

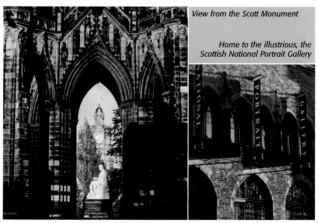

View from the Scott Monument

Home to the illustrious, the Scottish National Portrait Gallery

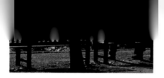

Georgian Facades of New Town

Explore New Town's streets and squares, full of superb Georgian architecture. For shopping try George Street and Multrees Walk.

DISTANCE: 4km (2.5 miles) **ALLOW:** 1 hour 30 minutes, plus stops

START

PRINCES STREET
✚ C5 🚌 3, 10, 17, 25, 44

① Start on Princes Street (▷ 74) by the Royal Scottish Academy (▷ 76). Cross over into Hanover Street. Take the second turning on your left and walk along George Street.

② At the end is Charlotte Square, one of the finest examples of Georgian architecture in the city. Turn right and right again into Young Street. At the end turn left and go down North Castle Street.

③ When you reach Queen Street cross over and turn left and then take the next right down Wemyss Place. Turn right into Heriot Row.

④ Here you will find the home of Robert Louis Stevenson. When you reach Howe Street turn left and take the second left into South East Circus Place.

END

PRINCES STREET
✚ C5 🚌 3, 10, 17, 25, 44

⑧ In front of you is St. Andrew Square. Go around the square, turning left into North St. David Street, which leads back to Princes Street.

⑦ At the roundabout turn right and walk up Broughton Street, with its good choice of refreshment stops. At the end of the street turn right onto York Place and then turn left into Elder Street. Take the next right down Multrees Walk (▷ 79, panel).

⑥ At the end turn right onto St. Vincent Street. Cross over into Great King Street and at the end turn right and then immediately left onto Drummond Place and continue ahead into London Street.

⑤ Pause to admire the sweep of the Royal Circus before you bear right for North East Circus Place.

Shopping

ANTHONY WOODD GALLERY

www.anthonywoodd.com
Traditional art—mainly 19th-century oils, watercolors and prints, from landscapes to caricatures and sporting and military subjects. Also excellent contemporary art.
➕ C4 ✉ 4 Dundas Street EH3 6HZ ☎ 0131 558 9544/5 🚌 13, 23, 27

ARKANGEL & FELON

www.arkangelandfelon.com
One of the popular fashion boutiques in this attractive street in the West End of the city, Arkangel & Felon is a delightful shop which sells exclusive designer clothes, unusual jewelry and accessories. There's also a selection of vintage evening wear, perfume and scented candles.
➕ A6 ✉ 4 William Street EH3 7NH ☎ 0131 226 4466 🚌 4, 12, 25

BELINDA ROBERTSON

www.belindarobertson.com
Scotland's renowned cashmere designer has come to the heart of Edinburgh's New Town. Belinda's creations, which include sweaters, gloves and scarves as well as cashmere knickers and G-strings, have been donned by the likes of Nicole Kidman and Madonna.
➕ C4 ✉ 13a Dundas Street EH3 6QG ☎ 0131 557 8118 🚌 13, 23, 27

DICKSON & MACNAUGHTON

www.dicksonandmacnaughton.com
For the archetypal country gentleman (or woman), this established store sells high-quality country clothing by all the leading manufacturers. It also stocks a full range of fishing and shooting accessories.
➕ C5 ✉ 21 Frederick Street EH2 2NE ☎ 0131 225 4218 🚌 24, 29, 42

FRASERS

www.houseoffraser.co.uk
This popular department store offers a comprehensive selection of clothes (including designer names like DKNY and Ralph Lauren), accessories, perfumes and kitchenware. There is a café on the fifth floor.
➕ D5 ✉ 145 Princes Street EH2 4YZ ☎ 0844 800 3724 🚌 3, 10, 17, 23, 24, 27, 44 and others

---

DESIGNER FASHION

Until not so long ago, Glasgow was considered to rule supreme over Edinburgh when it came to shopping for designer names. But now things have changed. Edinburgh is challenging its rival with stylish home-grown boutiques, international fashion outlets and top department stores. A string of designer names have extended their empires to Edinburgh.

HAMILTON & INCHES

www.hamiltonandinches.com
Established in 1866, the city's most reputable jeweler offers fine imaginative jewelry and silverware in a grand old building with workshops above and an ornate interior, complete with chandeliers.
➕ D5 ✉ 87 George Street EH2 3EY ☎ 0131 225 4898 🚌 13, 23, 24, 27, 29, 42

HARVEY NICHOLS

www.harveynichols.com
Scotland's first branch of this exclusive London department store added a touch of glamor when it opened in Edinburgh in 2002; perfumes, designer handbags, accessories and clothes, including Gucci, Burberry, Prada, Fendi and Dior. A bar, brasserie and top-floor restaurant add plenty of options for refreshment after hectic shopping.
➕ E4 ✉ 30–34 St. Andrew Square EH2 2AD ☎ 0131 524 8388 🚌 8, 10, 11, 12, 16

HECTOR RUSSELL

www.hector-russell.com
Part of a well-known chain of kilt shops, this branch allows you to rent as well as buy. It's all here, from a *sgian dubh* (small knife worn inside the sock) to the complete outfit. The shop will arrange for your purchases to be mailed home. Additional branch in High Street.
➕ D5 ✉ 95 Princes Street EH2 2ER ☎ 0131 220 2493;

freephone order number (UK only) 0800 980 4010 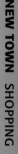 3, 10, 17, 25, 44

HELEN BATEMAN
www.helenbateman.com
For bona fide limited editions designed by the owner, visit this exclusive store that displays a superb range of shoes, boots and accessories that are unique and also affordable.
➕ A6 ✉ 16 William Street EH3 7NH ☎ 0131 220 4495 🚌 4, 12, 25

JANE DAVIDSON
www.janedavidson.co.uk
Jane's daughter Sarah has built her reputation on providing excellent service. The three-floor Georgian town house stocks exclusive cashmere labels from around the world and features many top designers, such as Allegra Hicks and Diane Von Furstenberg.
➕ C5 ✉ 52 Thistle Street EH2 1EN ☎ 0131 225 3280 🚌 23, 27, 29, 42

JENNERS
www.houseoffraser.co.uk
Edinburgh's grand old dame was founded in 1838 and occupies a magnificent building. The rabbit warren inside, with a central galleried arcade, houses over 100 departments, from clothes and shoes to perfume, glassware, groceries and toys. There are four cafés. Now owned by House of Fraser.
➕ E5 ✉ 48 Princes Street

Edinburgh EH2 2YJ ☎ 0844 800 3725 🚌 3, 10, 17, 23, 24, 27, 44 and others

JOSEPH BONNAR
www.josephbonnar.com
In business since the 1960s, Joseph Bonnar boasts Scotland's largest range of antique jewelry, plus other items.
➕ C5 ✉ 72 Thistle Street EH2 1EN ☎ 0131 226 2811 🚌 23, 27, 29, 42

KURT GEIGER
www.kurtgeiger.com
Shoes for men and women are beautifully displayed in this upscale shop in the designer shopping area, Multrees Walk. Brands range from Paul Smith and

WALK THE WALK
Multrees Walk is a great place for designer shopping in Edinburgh (www.the-walk. co.uk). The stylish pedestrianized shopping street has attracted a whole host of prestigious international retailers, such as Links of London, Mulberry, Azendi, Calvin Klein, Louis Vuitton, Emporio Armani and Boss. It also boasts a five-floor Harvey Nichols department store (▷ 78), several stylish accessory shops and galleries, and the excellent Valvona & Crolla Vincaffé bar and restaurant (▷ 86). For more affordable shopping go to the St. James Centre (▷ 80).

French Connection to Birkenstock, Ugg and Crocs, as well as Kurt Geiger's own styles.
➕ E4 ✉ Multrees Walk, St. Andrew Square EH1 3DQ ☎ 0131 556 1816 🚌 8, 10, 11, 12, 16

LINZI CRAWFORD
www.linzicrawford.com
The only stockist of several edgy European labels, along with Linzi's own line of merino and cashmere in distinct shades.
➕ D4 ✉ 27 Dublin Street EH3 6NL ☎ 0131 558 7558 🚌 13

MCNAUGHTAN'S BOOKSHOP
www.mcnaughtansbookshop. com
A highly respected secondhand and anti-quarian bookshop where casual browsing can sometimes unearth a real gem. The helpful owner, Elizabeth Strong, will search for specific titles.
➕ F4 ✉ 3a/4a Haddington Place, Leith Walk EH7 4AE ☎ 0131 556 5897 🚌 7, 10, 11, 12, 14, 16, 22, 25, 34, 49

MOLTON BROWN
www.moltonbrown.co.uk
The simple clean lines of this store are reflected in the products: pampering lotions and delectable fragrances for men and women.
➕ D5 ✉ 35a George Street EH2 2HN ☎ 0131 225 8452 🚌 13, 19, 37, 41

Entertainment and Nightlife

AMARONE
www.amaronerestaurant.co.uk
This stylish, bustling wine bar and restaurant in the heart of New Town has a good wine list and an Italian-inspired cocktail list. ✚ D4 ✉ 13 St. Andrew Square EH2 2BH ☎ 0131 523 1171 🕐 Mon–Fri 8am–10.30pm, Sat–Sun 10am–10.30pm 🚌 8, 10, 11, 12, 16 and tram (at St. Andrew Square)

ASSEMBLY ROOMS
www.assemblyrooms edinburgh.com
Elegant Georgian building showcasing mainstream Festival Fringe productions, with an impressive ballroom and music hall. ✚ C5 ✉ 54 George Street EH2 2LE ☎ 0131 220 4348 (box office) 🚌 24, 29, 42

BAILLIE BAR
Sample real ales at this New Town basement pub with an interesting triangular-shape bar and low ceilings. ✚ B3 ✉ 2–4 St. Stephen Street EH3 5AL ☎ 0131 225 4673 🕐 Mon–Thu 11am–midnight, Fri, Sat 11am–1am, Sun 12.30–midnight 🚌 19A, 24, 29, 42

THE BARONY
This fine old pub serves decent food and hosts live rock and blues most Saturday and Sunday nights. ✚ E3 ✉ 81–85 Broughton Street EH3 3RJ ☎ 0131 558 2873 🕐 Normal pub hours; live shows from 8.30 🚌 8

CAFÉ ROYAL
Stop for a drink and admire the ornate ceiling, tiled portraits, stained glass and mahogany carvings here. The huge bar takes center stage. ✚ E5 ✉ 19 West Register Street EH2 2AA ☎ 0131 556 1884 🕐 Mon–Wed 11–11, Thu 11am–midnight, Fri, Sat 11am–1am, Sun 12.30–11pm 🚌 3, 10, 17, 23, 24, 27, 44

CITY NIGHTCLUB
www.cityedinburgh.co.uk
This amazing sports bar and nightclub, in the basement of the Scotsman Hotel (entrance in New Town's Market Street), is Edinburgh's most talked about late-night venue.

THE GAY SCENE
Edinburgh has a vibrant gay scene that revolves around Broughton Street, an area known as the Pink Triangle. Hotels, clubs, cafés and pubs cater to the gay community. For pre-club drinks try The Basement (✉ 10a–12a Broughton Street EH1 3RH ☎ 0131 557 0097; www.basement-bar-edinburgh.co.uk) or The Street (✉ 2b Picardy Place EH1 3JT ☎ 0131 556 4272; thestreetbaredinburgh.co.uk). CC Blooms (✉ 23 Greenside Place EH1 3AA ☎ 0131 556 9331), is a popular gay rendezvous during the day and turns into a lively club-style venue at night, open till 3am.

✚ E6 ✉ 1a Market Street EH1 1DE ☎ 0131 226 9560 🕐 Wed, Fri, Sat to 3am 🚌 3, 5, 7, 30, 31, 33, 37

EDINBURGH PLAYHOUSE
www.livenationtheatres.co.uk
A multi-purpose auditorium in a former cinema that presents big-budget musicals and dance, and concerts featuring leading rock groups. Close to the east end of Princes Street. ✚ F4 ✉ 18–22 Greenside Place EH1 3AA ☎ 0131 524 3333, 0870 606 3424 (ticketmaster 24 hours) 🚌 7, 10, 11, 12, 14, 22, 25, 26, 49

JONGLEURS
www.jongleurs.com
With more than 20 years' experience and a host of well-known comedians passing through its doors, the Edinburgh branch of this chain of comedy clubs is always good for a laugh. ✚ F4 ✉ Unit 6/7 Omni Centre, Greenside Place EH1 3AA ☎ 0844 844 0044 (for bookings) 🕐 Times vary 🚌 7, 10, 11, 12, 14, 22, 25, 26

LOLALO
www.lolaloedinburgh.com
This Polynesian-style tiki bar and dance club has a list of some 30 potent cocktails and also serves fine champagnes and rums from around the world. It attracts a young, lively and free-spending clientele.

Clockwise from far left: on lookout, a meerkat stands guard at Edinburgh Zoo; checking out the giraffe enclosure; one of the zoo's most popular events, the Penguin Parade always attracts a big crowd; who's talking to who?—the penguin enclosure at Edinburgh Zoo; more penguins waddling through the zoo

hillocks occupied by the nyala antelope, and the African plains. Several other artfully designed enclosures give a sense of spaciousness, including the lion and tiger areas and the Budongo Trail, where you can see chimpanzees in a unique interactive enclosure. You can take a 30-minute free Hilltop Safari ride to the top of the zoo, with commentary on the animals on the way round.

Penguins and pandas In 2014 the zoo celebrated the centenary of the arrival of the first live penguins ever seen in Europe, shipped from South Georgia. The original penguin enclosure was modernized and expanded in 2013 and the daily Penguin Parade is one of the major attractions. However, since 2011 the penguins have been overshadowed by the zoo's two pandas, Tian Tian and Yang Guang.

THE BASICS

www.edinburghzoo.org.uk
✚ Off map at A7
✉ Corstorphine Road EH12 6TS
☎ 0131 334 9171
🕐 Apr–Sep daily 9–6; Oct, Mar daily 9–5; Nov–Feb daily 9–4.30
🍴 Restaurant, café, kiosks and picnic areas
🚌 12, 26, 31
♿ Very good
💷 Expensive

Leith

HIGHLIGHTS

- The Shore
- Ocean Terminal
- Water of Leith Visitor Centre
- Royal Yacht *Britannia*

TIP

- Choose a dry and, if possible, sunny day to visit Leith to get the most from the coastal location.

Edinburgh's seaport, amalgamated with the city in 1921, has been a dock area since the 14th century. Following a decline in shipbuilding, it has been regenerated into a trendy tourist area.

New role Leith was for many years a prosperous town in its own right. As the shipbuilding industry began to wane in the 20th century the town went into decline, but in recent years it has come up in the world, and now it buzzes with fashionable eating places. The area known as The Shore, along the waterfront, has been well restored and is filled with flourishing bars and restaurants. Warehouses, once full of wine and whisky, have been converted into smart accommodation. Where Tower Street meets The Shore, look for the Signal Tower, built in 1686 as a windmill. Edinburgh's river, the Water of Leith,

Clockwise from top left: take a cruise out from the waterside at Leith; The Shore restaurant and bar, Leith; working boats in Leith docks; new apartments at Leith are popular, especially with young city workers

flows through the middle of the town and the visitor center tells more about its wildlife and heritage.

Historic Leith The town has witnessed its share of history—Mary, Queen of Scots, landed here from France in 1561 and reputedly stayed at Andro Lamb's House, in Water Street. James II of Scotland banned golf from Leith links as it interfered with archery practice. The original 13 rules of golf were drawn up here in 1744, but in 1907 the dunes were flattened to create a public park and golf was banned once more.

Modern development For visitors, the Royal Yacht *Britannia* (▷ 97) is the draw, and to access the ship you enter through the Ocean Terminal Centre (▷ 104), one of Europe's largest shopping and leisure complexes, with a 12-screen cinema.

THE BASICS

🗺 Off map at H1

✉ Leith

🚌 1, 11, 16, 22, 34, 35, 36

ℹ Edinburgh and Scotland Information Centre, 3 Princes Street EH2 2QP

☎ 0845 225 5121

Royal Botanic Garden ⭐ TOP 25

The entrance gate to the gardens (left) and an orchid from the collection (right)

THE BASICS

www.rbge.org.uk
➕ A–B1 ✉ 20A Inverleith Row EH3 5LR
☎ 0131 552 7171
🕐 Apr–Sep daily 10–7; Mar, Oct daily 10–6; Nov–Feb daily 10–4
🍴 Gateway Restaurant and Terrace Café
🚌 8, 17, 23, 27
♿ Good
✋ Moderate charge for the glasshouses; tours moderate
❓ Tours lasting around 90 minutes leave West Gate at 11 and 2, Apr–Sep. Extensive Botanics gift shop with stationery, plants and related souvenirs

HIGHLIGHTS

- Rock Garden
- Glasshouses
- Tropical Aquatic House
- Chinese Hillside
- Scottish Heath Garden
- The gates
- Orchid and Cycad House
- Woodland Garden

Known locally as The Botanics, these gardens boast some 15,500 species, one of the largest collections of living plants in the world. It's possibly Edinburgh's finest recreational asset.

City greenery Occupying this site since 1823, the gardens cover more than 28ha (69 acres) of beautifully landscaped and wooded grounds to the north of the city, forming an immaculately maintained green oasis. You can walk to the garden from Princes Street via Stockbridge, though you may wish to take the bus back up the hill. It is especially suitable for children as it is dog-free.

Inside or out? There are 10 glasshouses to explore, offering a perfect haven on cold days. They include an amazingly tall palm house dating back to 1834, and the Tropical Aquatic House, with its giant waterlilies and an underwater view of fish swimming through the lily roots. Outside, the plants of the Chinese Hillside and the Heath Garden are particularly interesting, and in summer the herbaceous borders are breathtaking. Check out the rhododendron collection and the Rock Garden, which displays some 5,000 species and is best seen in May. The highest point of the garden has a fine view of the city.

Striking design The West Gate, or Carriage Gate, is the main entrance, but don't miss the stunning inner east side gates, designed by local architect Ben Tindall in 1996.

Royal Yacht *Britannia*

The Royal Yacht Britannia (left) has a full-size lounge within its hull (right)

This former royal yacht is one of the world's most famous ships, now moored in Edinburgh's historic port of Leith. It is 83rd in a long line of royal yachts stretching back to 1660.

New role *Britannia* was decommissioned in 1997 after a cut in government funds. It had carried the Queen and her family on 968 official voyages all over the world since its launch at Clydebank in 1953.

Vital statistics For 40 years, *Britannia* served the royal family, sailing more than 1 million miles to become the most famous ship in the world. A compact yacht, it is just 125.6m (412ft) long. It carried a crew of 240, including a Royal Marine band and an additional 45 household staff when the royal family were aboard. The onshore visitor area sets the scene, telling the history of the ship. A self-guided tour using handsets takes you around the yacht itself. *Britannia* still retains the fittings and furnishings of her working days, which gives an intimate insight into the royals away from usual palace protocol.

Royal and naval precision Check out the apartments adorned with hundreds of original items from the royal collection. The grandest room is the State Dining Room, and the most elegant the Drawing Room. Imagine the royal family relaxing in the Sun Lounge and view the modest sleeping quarters. Everything on board is shipshape, from the Engine Room to the fully equipped Sick Bay.

THE BASICS

www.royalyachtbritannia.co.uk

🚌 Off map at H1

✉ Ocean Terminal, Leith EH6 6JJ

☎ 0131 555 5566

🕐 Jan–Mar, Nov–Dec daily 10–3.30; Apr–Jun, Oct 9.30–4; Jul–Sep 9.30–4.30

🍴 Cafés and restaurants in Ocean Terminal

🚌 1, 11, 22, 34, 35, 36

♿ Excellent

💷 Expensive

❓ Reservations strongly advised in high season

HIGHLIGHTS

● Royal Apartments
● Drawing Room
● State Dining Room
● Sun Lounge
● Royal Bedrooms
● Sick Bay and Operating Theatre
● Engine Room
● The Bridge

Scottish National Gallery of Modern Art

Outside the gallery; Le Coureur (The Runner), by Germaine Richier

THE BASICS

www.nationalgalleries.org

🔲 Off map at A5

✉ 75 Belford Road
EH4 3DR

☎ 0131 624 6200

🕐 Daily 10–5

🍴 Gallery Café

🚌 13; free bus links all five national galleries

🚉 Edinburgh Haymarket

♿ Very good

💷 Free, but may be charges for temporary exhibitions

❓ Shop stocks books, cards, gifts

HIGHLIGHTS

● Works by the Scottish Colourists, including those by John Duncan Fergusson
● Major works by Picasso, Matisse and Lichtenstein
● Sculptures by Henry Moore and Barbara Hepworth
● Works by contemporary artists, including Damien Hirst and Rachel Whiteread

The gallery opened at this parkland site in 1984, providing an ideal setting for the work of those who have been in the forefront of modern art: Matisse, Picasso, Hirst—you'll find them all here.

Setting the scene The first thing you see as you arrive at the main gallery is a sweeping, living sculpture of grassy terraces and semicircular ponds, an installation called *Landform UEDA* by Charles Jencks. After such a grand introduction the rest of the gallery seems quite small, but it is certainly large in terms of its enviable and varied collection of modern art from around the world. It is housed in a former school.

On display Regularly changing exhibitions occupy the first floor, with a varied display from the gallery's collection on the second floor. Among these pieces, look for works by Picasso, Braque and Matisse, Hepworth and Gabo. The work of the early-20th-century group of painters known as the Scottish Colourists is particularly striking, with canvases by Samuel John Peploe (1871–1935), George Leslie Hunter (1877–1931), John Duncan Fergusson (1874–1961) and F.C.B. Cadell (1883–1937). Also of interest are Fergusson's dramatic *Portrait of Anne Estelle Rice* (c. 1908), the vibrancy of Cadell's *The Blue Fan* (c. 1922) and Peploe's later, more fragmentary work, such as *Iona Landscape, Rocks* (c. 1927).

More modern art Stroll across the road to the Dean Gallery (▷ 99), an outstation of the gallery.

More to See

ANN STREET

One of Edinburgh's most exclusive addresses is based on the estate built in 1814 by artist Sir Henry Raeburn in memory of his wife, Ann. Located between Stockbridge and New Town, the houses combine classic splendor with cottagey charm.

🏠 A4 ⊠ Ann Street 🚌 29, 37, 41, 42

BLACKFORD HILL

One of Edinburgh's seven hills, the view from here is excellent. Just 3km (2 miles) south of central Edinburgh, it is home to the Royal Scottish Observatory, which moved here from Calton Hill in 1895. The visitor area is open only for group visits and occasional events. There are Friday evening viewing sessions (book in advance; tel 0131 668 8404; www.darkskydiscovery.org.uk).

🏠 Off map at D9 ⊠ Blackford 🚌 24, 38, 41 ♿ Few

CRAMOND

There are Roman remains, 16th-century houses, a fine church, an old inn and some elegant Victorian villas to hold your attention in this attractive suburb on the shores of the Firth of Forth. The Cramond Heritage Trust has a permanent exhibition in the Maltings exploring the history of the village. Take one of the good walks around the area or visit Lauriston Castle (▷ 100), nearby.

🏠 Off map at A1 ⊠ Cramond
🕐 Maltings: Apr–Sep Sat, Sun 2–5; every afternoon during Festival 🚌 24, 41

DEAN GALLERY

www.nationalgalleries.org

Across the road from the Scottish National Gallery of Modern Art (▷ 98), this gallery is housed in a former orphanage and displays an excellent collection based around the work of Dada and the Surrealists, and the Scottish sculptor Eduardo Paolozzi (b.1924).

🏠 Off map at A5 ⊠ 73 Belford Road EH4 3DR ☎ 0131 624 6200 🕐 Daily 10–5 🚌 13; free bus linking main galleries 🚉 Edinburgh Haymarket ♿ Very good 💷 Free

Take in the view over Edinburgh from Blackford Hill

Rows of boats at Cramond waterside

DEAN VILLAGE

The northern limit of New Town is marked by Thomas Telford's 1832 Dean Bridge. It spans a steep gorge created by the Water of Leith. The workers' cottages, warehouses and mill buildings have been restored and Dean has become a desirable residential area. The cemetery is the resting place of many well-known locals, including the New Town architect William Playfair.

✚ Off map at A5 ✉ Dean 🚌 13, 37, 41

JUPITER ARTLAND

www.jupiterartland.org

This cutting-edge collection of contemporary landscape art and installations includes works by Charles Jencks, Andy Goldsworthy and the late Ian Hamilton Finlay, scattered around a 100-acre (40.5ha) estate surrounding Bonnington House.

✚ Off map at A8 ✉ Bonnington House Steadings, Wilkieston EH627 8BB C01506 889 900 🕐 May–Sep Thu–Sun 10–5 🚌 27 ✋ Adults: expensive; children: moderate

LAURISTON CASTLE

www.edinburghmuseums.org.uk

This "castle" is the epitome of Edwardian comfort and style, a gabled and turreted mansion overlooking the Firth of Forth near Cramond. Starting out as a simple tower house, it was renovated and extended several times and left to the City of Edinburgh in 1926 by William Robert Reid.

✚ Off map at A1 ✉ 2A Cramond Road South, Davidson's Mains EH4 5QD ☎ 0131 336 2060 🕐 Apr–Oct Sat–Thu tours at 11, 12, 2, 3, 4; Nov–Mar Sat, Sun at 12, 2, 3. Grounds open 9am–dusk 🚌 24 ♿ Good ✋ Castle: moderate. Grounds: free

MORNINGSIDE

Immortalized in the accent of novelist Muriel Spark's Jean Brodie, this southwest suburb still houses the wealthy of the city. A quiet leafy spot graced with Victorian villas, it still oozes gentility. Stroll round its pleasant streets for civilized shopping and afternoon tea.

✚ Off map at B9 ✉ Morningside 🚌 5, 11, 15, 15A, 16, 17, 23, 41

Buildings at Dean village, on the banks of the Water of Leith

Entertainment and Nightlife

ALIEN ROCK

www.alienrock.co.uk
Scotland's leading indoor rock-climbing center, Alien Rock, takes advantage of the cavernous interior of a former church to offer challenging roped climbs on an artificial wall. Great for both beginners and experienced climbers.
🚇 Off map ✉ 8 Pier Place EH6 4LP ☎ 0131 552 7211 🚌 7, 16

CHURCH HILL THEATRE

Mainly amateur productions but professionals perform here during the Festival.
🚇 Off map ✉ 33a Morningside Road EH10 4RR ☎ 0131 447 7597 🚌 5, 11, 15, 16, 17, 23

DOMINION

www.dominioncinemas.net
This old-fashioned, family-run cinema is the ideal antidote to the multiplex cinemas in the city. View latest releases in leather Pullman seats, or indulge in the Gold Class service, which offers leather sofas with complimentary wine or beer and snacks.
🚇 Off map ✉ 18 Newbattle Terrace, Morningside EH10 4RT ☎ 0131 447 4771 (box office) 🚌 11, 15, 16, 23

EDINBURGH CORN EXCHANGE

www.ece.uk.com
Acts here have included well-known bands such as Blur, Travis and Coldplay.
🚇 Off map ✉ 11 Newmarket Road EH14 1RJ ☎ 0131 447 3500 🚌 35 🚉 Slateford from Waverley

FOOTBALL

Edinburgh's two main professional teams are Heart of Midlothian (Hearts) and Hibernian (Hibs), who play in the Scottish Premier League. They are at home on alternate Saturday afternoons Aug–May (reserve in advance).
Hearts FC 🚇 Off map ✉ Tynecastle Stadium, McLeod Street EH11 2NL ☎ 0871 663 1874; www.heartsfc.co.uk 🚌 3, 3a, 25, 33
Hibs FC 🚇 Off map ✉ Easter Road Stadium, 12 Albion Place EH7 5QG ☎ 0844 844 1875; www.hiberianfc..co.uk 🚌 1

HORSE RACING

www.musselburgh-racecourse.co.uk
Musselburgh Racecourse, one of the best small racecourses in Britain, hosts 26 flat and jump meetings a year.
🚇 Off map ✉ Linkfield Road, Musselburgh, East Lothian EH21 7RG ☎ 0131 665 2859 🚌 15, 15A

ODEON WESTER HAILES

www.odeon.co.uk
This modern complex, opposite a shopping center on the outskirts of Edinburgh, has 12 screens showing a range of mainstream movies.
🚇 Off map ✉ 120 Wester Hailes Road EH14 3HR ☎ 0871 224 4007 🚌 30, 33 🚉 Wester Hailes from Haymarket

RUGBY

(▷ 101 for Murrayfield.)

SWIMMING

Edinburgh is proud of its Olympic-size indoor swimming pool, complete with a diving pool and waterslides. Royal Commonwealth Pool
🚇 H9 ✉ 21 Dalkeith Road EH16 5BB ☎ 0131 667 7211 🚌 2, 14, 30, 33

VUE

www.myvue.com
All the latest releases are shown at this state-of-the-art 12-screen multiplex, with comfortable seats and the latest in digital surround sound. Free parking.
🚇 Off map ✉ Ocean Terminal, Ocean Drive, Leith EH6 6JJ ☎ 0871 224 0240 🚌 1, 11, 22, 34, 35

GOLF

Golf is the national game and with more than 500 courses throughout the country, it's no wonder fanatics flock to the area in pursuit of their first love. The closest courses can be found at Braids Hill, Craigmillar Park and Silverknowes. Visit www.scottishgolf.com for a list of courses in the area and a reservation service.

Restaurants

PRICES

Prices are approximate, based on a 3-course meal for one person.

£££ over £25
££ £15–£25
£ under £15

A ROOM IN LEITH (£££)

www.aroomin.co.uk/leith
This is a pretty quayside restaurant in a former lockkeeper's cottage. Fresh, well-prepared Scottish produce is featured in the fish, meat and vegetarian dishes that are served in intimate booths or in the conservatory. Expect a warm welcome.
🚇 Off map ✉ 1c Dock Place, Leith EH6 6LU
☎ 0131 554 7427
⏰ Lunch, dinner 🚌 16, 22, 35, 36

RESTAURANT AT THE BONHAM (£££)

www.thetownhousecompany.com
In the boutique West End hotel The Bonham (▷ 112), long windows, wooden floors and chic brown-and-cream livery set the scene for stylish, contemporary cooking. Desserts such as orange blossom panacotta with lavender *tuile* are almost too attractive to eat.
🚇 Off map ✉ Bonham Hotel, 35 Drumsheugh Gardens EH3 7RN ☎ 0131 274 7444 ⏰ Lunch, dinner
🚌 13

RESTAURANT MARTIN WISHART (£££)

www.restaurantmartinwishart.co.uk
Michelin-starred Martin Wishart's dishes are beautifully presented at this tiny French restaurant on the waterfront at Leith. Bright, modern art stands out against the white walls and stone floors.
🚇 Off map ✉ 54 The Shore, Leith EH6 6RA
☎ 0131 553 3557
⏰ Lunch, dinner; closed Sun, Mon 🚌 16, 22, 35, 36

RHUBARB (£££)

www.prestonfield.com
The food more than matches the opulent setting at this hotel. Don't miss the rhubarb crème brûlée. You will need to take a taxi to get here, but it's worth the effort.

SCOTTISH SALMON

Scottish salmon is celebrated as being among the best in the world, but be aware of the variation between wild (caught) and farmed salmon. In the past, salmon farming has been hard hit by controversy about fish kept in overcrowded sea cages, the use of dye to tint the flesh, and the presence of various chemicals and pollutants. Many salmon farmers have changed their ways, but many restaurants still consider wild salmon to be superior.

🚇 Off map ✉ Prestonfield Hotel, Priestfield Road EH16 5UT ☎ 0131 225 1333
⏰ Lunch, dinner

SHIP ON THE SHORE (£££)

www.theshipontheshore.co.uk
Tasty seafood options at this bistro-style bar may include smoked salmon with lemon, chopped onion and capers, or paupiette of sole and prawns on braised leeks.
🚇 Off map ✉ 24–26 The Shore, Leith EH6 6QN
☎ 0131 555 0409 ⏰ Lunch, dinner 🚌 16, 22, 35, 36

SHORE BAR & RESTAURANT (££)

www.fishersbistros.co.uk
This informal, zesty establishment in an 18th-century building serves fresh, succulent fish in its French-brasserie-style dining room overlooking the Water of Leith.
🚇 Off map ✉ 3 The Shore, Leith EH6 6QW ☎ 0131 553 5080 ⏰ Lunch, dinner
🚌 16, 22, 35, 36

STARBANK INN (££)

www.starbankinn-edinburgh.co.uk
On the waterfront, this inn offers traditional pub food, such as roast lamb with mint sauce, poached salmon, or chicken with tarragon cream sauce, and great views over the Firth of Forth.
🚇 Off map ✉ 64 Laverockbank Road EH5 3BZ
☎ 0131 552 4141 ⏰ Lunch, dinner 🚌 7, 10, 11, 16

Edinburgh has a diverse range of accommodations on offer, from opulent five-star hotels to lovely, if more humble, Georgian guesthouses. Scottish hospitality is in abundance throughout the city.

Introduction

It is important to reserve well in advance if you are considering visiting Edinburgh during Festival time or over Hogmanay for the New Year's celebrations. In the quieter times of year you'll find some bargain deals.

What the Grades Mean

You may notice that displayed outside all Scottish accommodation is a blue plaque with a thistle symbol. This indicates the star rating issued by VisitScotland (the Scottish Tourist Board). Every type of accommodation is assessed annually and awarded anything from one to five stars to indicate the quality of accommodations, cleanliness, ambience, hospitality, service, food and facilities offered.

En Suite

Bed-and-breakfast accommodation offers the opportunity to stay in somebody's home, and sometimes in some remarkable historical buildings. Be aware that en-suite facilities are not always available and bathrooms may be shared. If a choice of bath or shower is important to you, check at the time of booking.

Paying

Some hotels will ask for a deposit or full payment in advance, especially for one-night bookings. Some will not take bookings for stays of only one night. Most hotels accept the majority of British and international credit cards, but be aware some smaller guesthouses or B&Bs may not take cards, so check when booking.

Hotels in Edinburgh come in many guises, often in beautiful old buildings

---

BED-AND-BREAKFAST

The B&B price generally includes a full cooked breakfast, which in Scotland may consist of any combination of porridge, eggs, fried bread, potato scones, sausage, bacon, mushrooms and tomatoes. Black pudding is often a traditional option, too. Lighter alternatives are usually available. Some establishments offer an evening meal, but you might need to order in advance. While hotels, inns and some guesthouses will have a license to serve alcohol, few bed-and-breakfasts do.

Budget Hotels

ABBOTSFORD GUEST HOUSE

www.abbotsfordguesthouse.co.uk

Just north of New Town, this family-run guesthouse has eight well-equipped bedrooms. Breakfast is taken at individual tables in the elegant dining room.

Off map ⊠ 36 Pilrig Street EH6 5AL ☎ 0131 554 2706 🚌 11

BELFORD HOSTEL

www.edinburghhostels.com

One of several Edinburgh hostels run by the same group, this one is west of New Town in a converted church. Good-quality accommodation for students and backpackers, with space for up to 98 guests in dorms, triple, double or family rooms.

Off map ⊠ 6–8 Douglas Gardens, Belford Road EH3 3DA ☎ 0131 202 6107 🚌 13

BONNINGTON GUEST HOUSE

www.thebonnington guesthouse.com

The owners extend a warm welcome at this delightful Victorian house not far from Leith, with seven bedrooms finished to a high standard and retaining original features.

Off map ⊠ 202 Ferry Road EH6 4NW ☎ 0131 554 7610 🚌 7, 11, 14

DENE GUEST HOUSE

www.deneguesthouse.com

Hospitable owners offer a comfortable stay and a good breakfast at this clean and tidy Georgian town house. Well sited in New Town—ideal for visiting the main sights.

C2 ⊠ 7 Eyre Place EH3 5ES ☎ 0131 556 2700 🚌 23, 27, 36

ELDER YORK GUESTHOUSE

www.elderyork.co.uk

This charming guesthouse on the upper floors of a listed Georgian build-ing offers superb value for money. You get a wee dram on the house on arrival, and the full Scottish breakfast will set you up for the day.

E3 ⊠ 38 Elder Street EH1 3DX ☎ 0131 556 1926 🚌 10, 11, 12, 16, 26, 44 and tram

EXPRESS BY HOLIDAY INN: CITY CENTRE

www.ichotelsgroup.com

Well positioned for New Town, Princes Street and all the shops, this hotel is opposite several theaters and the Omni Leisure Centre. The 161 rooms are clean and practical. A continental-style buffet breakfast is included.

F4 ⊠ Picardy Place EH1 3JT ☎ 0131 558 2300 🚌 1, 4, 5, 8, 11, 12, 16, 17, 19, 25, 26, 45

IVY HOUSE

www.ivyguesthouse.com

A pretty Victorian guesthouse south of the city. The eight bedrooms come in various sizes. Good, substantial breakfasts.

Off map ⊠ 7 Mayfield Gardens EH9 2AX ☎ 0131 667 3411 🚌 3, 7, 8, 29, 31, 37, 49

TRAVELODGE EDINBURGH CENTRAL

www.travelodge.co.uk

Travelodge has 193 good-quality, spacious rooms in a central location, making it ideal for families.

F6 ⊠ 33 St. Mary's Street EH1 1TA ☎ 0871 984 6137 🚌 35, 36

SYHA

The Scottish Youth Hostels Association (SYHA) offers self-catering accommodation hostel-style all over Scotland. In central Edinburgh you can stay at the only five-star hostel in the city, run by the SYHA. Edinburgh Central Hostel is minutes from Waverley Station and Princes Street. It is suitable for individuals, families and groups. There are single, twin and eight-bed rooms and all are en suite. It has a bistro, and self-catering facilities are also available. It's an inexpensive way to be in the heart of the city (⊠ 9 Haddington Place EH7 4AL ☎ 0131 524 2090; www.syha.org.uk).

Mid-Range Hotels

PRICES

Expect to pay between £75 and £150 per night for a double room in a mid-range hotel.

APEX CITY HOTEL

www.apexhotels.co.uk
A modern, stylish hotel in a historic and fashionable square dominated by Edinburgh Castle above. There are 119 fresh, contemporary rooms. Drinks and meals can be taken in the Agua Bar and Restaurant, a smart open-plan area in dark wood and chrome. Guests can use the spa at the nearby International Hotel.
🞥 D7 ⊠ 61 Grassmarket EH1 2JF ☎ 0131 365 0000 (outside UK 0044 131 441 0440) 🚌 2

THE BALLANTRAE

www.ballantraehotel.co.uk
This hotel, in a listed Georgian town house in New Town, is in the lower end of the mid-range price bracket. The 19 spacious rooms have period detail. The honeymoon suite has a four-poster bed and the family room has a Jacuzzi. Next door, the Ballantrae Apartments offer self-catering in one- or two-bedroom apartments, providing an independent way of visiting the city.
🞥 E4 ⊠ 8 York Place EH1 3EP ☎ 0131 478 4748 🚌 4, 8, 10, 11, 12, 15, 16, 17, 26, 44, 45

BRUNTSFIELD HOTEL

www.thebruntsfield.co.uk
Overlooking Bruntsfield Links, this Best Western hotel has stylish lounge areas and 67 bedrooms, varying in size. Meals are served in a conservatory-style restaurant and there's an imaginative choice of lunch and dinner menus, using locally sourced ingredients.
🞥 B9 ⊠ 69–74 Bruntsfield Place EH10 4HH ☎ 0131 229 1393 🚌 11, 15, 16, 17, 23

ACCOMMODATION

Apart from the larger more obvious hotels, Edinburgh has numerous guesthouses and small family-run hotels. The latter will have more rooms, normally all with en-suite facilities; they will probably be licensed to serve alcohol and they will provide breakfast, dinner and sometimes lunch. For something more homelike, bed-and-breakfasts are usually very comfortable, and give you the opportunity to sample a real Scottish breakfast (▷ 108). If you intend to stay outside the city and just go in for individual days to sight-see, it can be worth considering self-catering accommodation (▷ 111, panel). There are several holiday parks nearby that offer holiday homes and touring caravan and camping pitches for the lower budget.

CHANNINGS

www.channings.co.uk
Elegant town house, once the home of Antarctic explorer Sir Ernest Shackleton, offering country-style tranquility in a West End setting. The 41 rooms vary in size but all are decorated with style.
🞥 Off map ⊠ South Learmonth Gardens EH4 1EZ ☎ 0131 560 2066 🚌 19, 37, 37A

DALMAHOY HOTEL MARRIOTT & COUNTRY CLUB

www.marriott.co.uk
An imposing Georgian mansion in beautiful parkland, 11km (7 miles) southwest of the city. Most of the 215 spacious bedrooms have great views of the Pentland Hills. Guests can use two golf courses, a pool, tennis facilities and a health and beauty club.
🞥 Off map ⊠ Kirknewton EH27 8EB ☎ 0131 333 1845

DUNSTANE HOUSE

www.dunstane-hotel-edinburgh.co.uk
In the city's West End close to Haymarket station, this 1850s Victorian mansion house has retained much of its architectural grandeur, giving a country-house atmosphere. Some of the 16 bedrooms have four-poster beds.
🞥 Off map ⊠ 4 West Coates, Haymarket EH12 5JQ ☎ 0131 337 6169 🚌 12, 26, 31

EDINBURGH CITY HOTEL

www.edinburghcityhotel.com
On a site that was once a maternity hospital, this tasteful conversion is close to central Edinburgh. The 52 spacious bedrooms are smartly modern and well equipped, with fridges. There is a cosy, yet stylish, bar and restaurant.
➕ D7 ✉ 79 Lauriston Place EH3 9HZ ☎ 0131 622 7979 🚌 2

GERALD'S PLACE

www.geraldsplace.com
Delightfully located opposite 200-year-old private gardens, this luxury bed-and-breakfast in a Georgian terrace has just two double rooms, with private bathrooms. Guests will be given Gerald's personal attention to ensure a perfect stay. A delicious full Scottish breakfast, using mostly organic produce, is included.
➕ D4 ✉ 21b Abercromby Place EH3 6QE ☎ 0131 558 7017 🚌 8, 10, 11, 12, 16

HOLYROOD HOTEL

www.macdonaldhotels.co.uk
This impressive business hotel, just a couple of minutes' walk from the Royal Mile and the new Scottish Parliament Building, offers extensive facilities, including conference suites and a spa. There are 156 rooms.
➕ G6 ✉ Holyrood Road EH8 6AE ☎ 0844 879 9028 🚌 35

HOTEL DU VIN

www.hotelduvin.com
This classy hotel, which opened in December 2008, is at the top end of this price bracket but it's worth looking for one of the good deals available. This former city asylum has 47 rooms and suites and offers a high level of comfort and decoration. First-class food is served in the hallmark Du Vin bistro, which has a whisky snug for relaxation.
➕ E7 ✉ Bristo Place, 2 Forrest Road EH1 1EY ☎ 0844 736 4255 🚌 2, 41, 42, 67

KEW HOUSE

www.kewhouse.com
Forming part of a listed Victorian terrace, Kew House is spotless

SELF-CATERING

If you are planning to stay outside Edinburgh and travel into the city daily, it is worth considering renting self-catering accommodation. The choice is good—you could stay in anything from an idyllic cottage to the wing of a castle. Even in Edinburgh itself, there are self-catering options available. The Edinburgh and Lothian Tourist Board publishes full details of self-catering options in its annual accommodation guide and also provides a reservation service.

throughout and has six bright bedrooms and a comfortable lounge offering supper and snack options. It's located near Murrayfield Stadium and is just a 15-minute walk from the center of Edinburgh. No smoking.
➕ Off map ✉ 1 Kew Terrace, Murrayfield EH12 5JE ☎ 0131 313 0700 🚌 12, 26, 31

MELVILLE CASTLE

www.melvillecastle.com
If you want to stay outside the city, try this castellated mansion in 20ha (50 acres) of wooded grounds 13km (8 miles) to the south. Impressively refurbished and complemented by good meals served in the vaulted cellar bar and brasserie. The hotel was once the hunting seat of Mary, Queen of Scots.
➕ Off map ✉ Melville Gate, Gilmerton Road EH18 1AP ☎ 0131 654 0088 🚌 3

LE MONDE

www.lemondehotel.co.uk
This should really be in the expensive range, but you can just squeeze the club-class room rate into the mid-range category and this stylish boutique hotel does some good out-of-season deals. All 18 rooms are themed on cities from around the globe. There's also a bar, brasserie and nightclub.
➕ D5 ✉ 16 George Street EH2 2PF ☎ 0131 270 3900 🚌 13, 19, 37, 41

Planning Ahead

When to Go

Edinburgh lies on the eastern side of Scotland, which is cooler, windier and drier than the west. At any time of year you are likely to meet rain, but the chances are it will not last for long. Some tourist sights close in winter, but major city museums stay open year-round.

AVERAGE DAILY MAXIMUM TEMPERATURES											
JAN	FEB	MAR	APR	MAY	JUN	JUL	AUG	SEP	OCT	NOV	DEC
39°F	39°F	43°F	48°F	54°F	61°F	63°F	61°F	59°F	54°F	45°F	41°F
4°C	4°C	6°C	9°C	12°C	16°C	17°C	16°C	15°C	12°C	7°C	5°C

Spring (March to May) has the best chance of clear skies and sunny days.

Summer (June to August) is unpredictable—it may be hot and sunny, but it can also be cloudy and wet. This is the time you can get *haar* (sea mist) that shrouds the city in thick mist, although this can happen at other times of the year as well.

Autumn (September to November) is usually more settled and there's a good chance of fine weather, but nothing is guaranteed.

Winter (December to February) can be cold, dark, wet and dreary, but there are also sparkling, clear, sunny days of frost, when the light is brilliant.

WHAT'S ON

January Burns Night (25 Jan): the birthday of Scotland's bard, celebrated throughout with haggis and whisky.

March/April Edinburgh Science Festival: science and technology events at various venues.

Ceilidh Culture: events centered around traditional Scottish arts.

May Bank of Scotland Imaginate Festival: Britain's largest performing arts festival for young people.

June Edinburgh International Film Festival: (▷ 41).

Royal Highland Show: Scotland's biggest agricultural show.

Edinburgh Marathon.

July/August Edinburgh Jazz & Blues Festival: 10 days of jazz performed by big names and new talent.

August Edinburgh International Festival: over three weeks, some of the world's best plays, opera, music and dance.

Edinburgh Festival Fringe: A chance for the amateurs to join the professionals.

Edinburgh Military Tattoo: (▷ 5).

International Book Festival: occupies a tented village in Charlotte Square.

Mela: a vibrant celebration of cultural diversity with music, dance and street performers.

October Scottish International Storytelling Festival: attracts storytellers from home and abroad.

November/December Edinburgh's Christmas: German and Scottish Christmas markets, ice rink, Ferris wheel and more.

December/January Edinburgh Hogmanay: (▷ 13).

Useful Websites

www.visitscotland.com
The official VisitScotland website, with a comprehensive database of information covering everything from weather, transport and events to shopping, nightlife and accommodations throughout Scotland.

www.eif.co.uk
A comprehensive guide to What's On at the Edinburgh International Festival.

www.edinburghguide.com
An informative guide to attractions, entertainment, recreation, eating out and accommodation, plus links to other sites.

www.nms.ac.uk
The National Museum of Scotland looks after many of Scotland's important museum collections. Its website provides detailed information about the museums in its care.

www.undiscoveredscotland.co.uk
An online guide to Scotland. The Edinburgh section has many useful links to other good sources of information.

www.nts.org.uk
The National Trust for Scotland looks after historic buildings in Scotland, including some in Edinburgh. Its website gives updated information about all the properties it is responsible for.

www.historic-scotland.gov.uk
This website has information on more than 300 listed buildings and ancient sites safeguarded by Historic Scotland.

www.list.co.uk
The website of Scotland's leading events, food, drink and entertainment listings magazine includes reviews of restaurants, cafés and bars and a comprehensive, up-to-the-minute guide to nightlife, film, theater, music and dance.

PRIME TRAVEL SITES

www.fodors.com
A complete travel-planning site. You can research prices and weather; reserve air tickets, cars and rooms; pose questions to (and get answers from) fellow visitors; and find links to other sites.

www.theAA.com
The AA's site helps you to find accommodations in the city, as well as pubs and restaurants.

ONLINE ACCESS

Free WiFi access is available at many cafés and bars throughout the city center (including branches of Caffe Nero and Costa Coffee) and in almost all hotels and guesthouses. Surprisingly, some larger hotels belonging to international chains still charge extra for WiFi in bedrooms—a service that most smaller places provide free.

Getting There

ENTRY REQUIREMENTS

● Visitors from outside the UK must have a passport, valid for at least six months from the date of entry.

● Before traveling, visitors from outside the UK should check visa requirements. See www.ukvisas.gov.uk or www.usembassy.org.uk/scotland.

● Photographic ID is required for all flights. Only passports are accepted.

CUSTOMS

● EU nationals do not have to declare goods imported for their own use, although you may be questioned by customs officials if you have large amounts of certain items.

● The limits for non-EU visitors are 200 cigarettes or 50 cigars or 250g of tobacco; 1 liter of alcohol (over 22 percent alcohol) or 2 liters of wine; 50g of perfume.

AIRPORTS

There are direct flights to Edinburgh's international airport from other parts of the UK and from continental Europe. United flies direct from Chicago and Air Canada flies direct from Toronto. Several airlines fly direct from North America to Glasgow International Airport (www.glasgowairport.com), which is around 90 minutes from Edinburgh by coach, train or car.

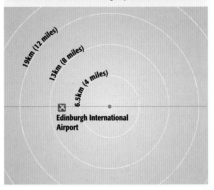

19km (12 miles)
13km (8 miles)
6.5km (4 miles)
Edinburgh International Airport

FROM EDINBURGH INTERNATIONAL AIRPORT

Edinburgh International Airport (www.edinburghairport.com; tel: 0844 448 883) is 20–30 minutes from the city center by bus, tram or cab. The new tram line runs between the airport to York Place, with intermediate stops at Murrayfield, Haymarket Station and along Princes Street. Airlink 100 buses operate between the airport and Waverley Bridge, in the city center, every 10 minutes and cost £4 one way or £7 round trip. The airport cab rank is opposite the Arrivals Hall, on the ground floor of the parking garage. The cab fare to the city center is £20–£30. Service 35 buses leave from stand 21, outside the Arrivals Hall, for Ocean Terminal in Leith. Stops include the Scottish Parliament and the Palace of Holyroodhouse: flat fare is £1.50. The N22 night bus also leaves from the stand outside the Arrivals Hall and runs from the airport to the city center and Ocean Terminal in Leith. Journey time is around 45 minutes: flat fare is £3.

INTERNAL FLIGHTS

Within the UK and Ireland, you can fly from Edinburgh to Belfast, Birmingham, Cardiff, Cork, Derry, Dublin, East Midlands, Exeter, Kirkwall, Knock, London (City, Gatwick, Heathrow, Luton and Stansted), Manchester, Newquay, Norwich, Shannon, Southampton, Southend, Stornoway and Sumburgh.

ARRIVING BY RAIL

Edinburgh has two major rail stations: Edinburgh Haymarket and Edinburgh Waverley. Waverley is a main hub for travel within Scotland, and has tourist information desks and other facilities. Regular trains connect Edinburgh with England, via the West Coast Main Line or East Coast Main Line. Most internal services are run by First ScotRail (www.firstgroup.com/scotland). For further details of fares and services contact the National Rail Enquiry Service (☎ 08457 484950; www.nationalrail.co.uk).

ARRIVING BY COACH

Coaches arrive in Edinburgh from England, Wales and all over Scotland at the St. Andrew Street bus station. The main coach companies operating to and from here are National Express (☎ 08717 818181; www.nationalexpress.com) and Scottish Citylink (☎ 08705 505050; www.citylink.co.uk). There is a taxi rank on St. David Street which can be accessed directly from the arrivals concourse.

ARRIVING BY CAR

One-way systems, narrow streets, "red" routes and dedicated bus routes make driving in the city difficult. Limited on-street parking is mostly pay-and-display 8.30am–6.30pm Mon–Sat. There are designated parking areas, to the south of Princes Street; the biggest is at Greenside Place, off Leith Street. Petrol stations are normally open Mon–Sat 6am–10pm, Sun 8am–8pm, though some (often self-service) are open 24 hours. All take credit cards and many have well-stocked shops.

NEED TO KNOW GETTING THERE

Getting Around

BY BUS AND TRAM

Edinburgh's urban bus network (www.lothianbuses.com) is excellent, reaching every part of the city and beyond. A flat-fare, one-way ride costs £1.50 for an adult, £0.70 for children 5–11 years, under 5 free. For a longer stay, buy a pack of 20 Citysingle tickets (£30 adult, £14 5–11 years, under 5 free) online from www.lothianbuses.com or at the city center Travelshop at Waverley Bridge. For overseas visitors, the tram is an excellent option for travel between the airport and city center. A one-way tram trip within the city center costs £1.50 (children 5–11 years £0.70, under 5 free). The one-way ride to the airport costs £5.00 (5–11 years £2.50).

TICKETS

Timetables and tickets are available at the Travel Shops (✉ 27 Hanover Street; Shandwick Place; Waverley Bridge ☎ Mon–Sat 8.15–6; Waverley Bridge also Sun 9.30–5.15). An enlarged map and timetable on the bridge outside Waverley Station has additional information about the night bus service into the suburbs.

TAXIS

Licensed taxis operate a reliable service day and night; fares are metered and strictly regulated. Cabs can be found at designated ranks like Waverley Bridge, can be hailed along the road, or called by phone (City Cabs ☎ 0131 228 1211; Central Radio Taxis ☎ 0131 229 2468).

CAR RENTAL

The major international car rental brands have desks at the airport, just outside the main Arrivals Hall. Several have city-center outlets. Some (including Hertz and Enterprise) advertise these as being located at Waverley Station but they may be a short walk away, on or near Picardy Place at the top of Leith Walk. If you plan on renting a car, choose accommodations that offers private car parking—it's almost impossible to find free parking space in most of the city.

EDINBURGH PASS

This card gives free access to more than 30 attractions in Edinburgh and the Lothians. It also includes free bus travel, including airport bus transfer, and special offers from some shops, restaurants and Festival events. A free guidebook explains what's on offer. Cost: 1-day pass £24, 2-day £36 and 3-day £48 (www.edinburghpass.com).

ORGANIZED SIGHTSEEING

A guided tour is a good way to gain more in-depth knowledge about Edinburgh. If time is short, take one of the open-top buses that wind their way around the city sights; all tours depart from Waverley Bridge and there are four types to choose from, including one where you can hop on and hop off at your leisure (☎ 0131 554 4494; www.edinburghtour. com). Entertaining and informative commentary is available in a number of languages. Various companies offer coach tours in and around the city. Try Rabbie's Trail Burners (☎ 0131 226 3133; www.rabbies.com), who run mini-coach (16-seater) tours to destinations such as Loch Ness and St. Andrews. For those who prefer two wheels, another option is Edinburgh Bike Tours (☎ 07753 136676; www.edinburghbiketours.co.uk), which offers full-day and half-day guided tours with all equipment provided.

WALKING TOURS

Mercat Walking Tours:
Walks where you explore secret underground vaults, ghost walks and fascinating history tours with dramatic commentaries, giving a true sense of Edinburgh's past and its people. ✉ Mercat House, 28 Blair Street EH1 1QR ☎ 0131 225 5445; www.mercattours.com
Sandemans New Edinburgh Tours:
A free, year-round, three-hour walking tour. www.newedinburghtours.com ☎ Leaves daily at 11 and 1 from in front of Starbucks Café by Tron Kirk on High Street.

VISITORS WITH DISABILITIES

● Capability Scotland (✉ 11 Ellersly Road, Edinburgh EH12 6HY ☎ 0131 337 9876; www.capability-scotland.org.uk) can advise on travel requirements to ensure a smooth trip.

● www.disabledgo.com is an internet service giving access information to people with disabilities, as well as other advice useful when visiting Edinburgh. Restaurants, cafés, shops and attractions are all covered.

● A wide range of information for visitors with disabilities can be found in VisitScotland's publication *Practical Information for Visitors with Disabilities*, available from the tourist board or from tourist offices.

STUDENT VISITORS

● Students can get reduced-cost entry to some museums and attractions by showing a valid student card.

● Budget accommodation is available (▷ 109).

● There are reduced fares on buses and trains for under 16s.

NEWSPAPERS AND MAGAZINES

● *The Scotsman* is at the quality end of the market.

● Scotland's popular tabloid daily newspaper is the *Daily Record.*

● *The Sunday Post* is a top-selling institution.

● *Scotland on Sunday* is a heavyweight that vies with the *Sunday Herald* for the more serious readership.

● *The List* is a lively fort-nightly listings magazine, giving excellent coverage for Edinburgh.

● Newspapers from around the world, including foreign-language papers, can be purchased at airports, larger train stations and some newspaper shops.

TELEPHONE SERVICES

● Various companies offer Directory Enquiries services. The British Telecom numbers are:

● Directory Enquiries
☎ 118 500

● International Directory Enquiries ☎ 118 505

● International Operator
☎ 155

● Operator ☎ 100

POST OFFICES

● Main post office ✉ St. James Centre, St. Andrew Square ☎ 0845 722 3344 🕐 Mon–Sat 9–5.30. Most other post offices open 9–12 on Sat.

● Many newspaper shops and supermarkets sell stamps.

● Postboxes are painted red; collection times are shown on each box.

RADIO AND TELEVISION

● Scotland is served by UK national radio stations and most Scottish regions and cities also have their own stations for local coverage. Edinburgh's is Radio Forth (97.3FM), which broadcasts a mix of news, music, traffic reports and weather forecasts.

● BBC Radio Scotland (94.3FM) broadcasts a similar mix but covers the whole of Scotland.

● Digital and satellite TV stations available in Scotland include all BBC national channels, ITV, STV, CNN and Sky channels.

TELEPHONES

● The code for Edinburgh is 0131. There is a full list of area codes and country codes in all phone books. Omit the area code when making a local call.

● Payphones are hard to find and the traditional red phone box is almost extinct. Payphones can be found at the airport, coach station, railway stations and elsewhere in the city center. They accept 10p, 20p, 50p and £1. Credit and debit cards can also be used. BT (British Telecom) payphones cost a minimum 60p for cash pay-ments and £1.20 when paying by card; the minimum charge includes a 40p connection charge and two calling time units of 10p.

● Mobile phone coverage is good but not all US and Canadian cell phones will work in the UK, and roaming charges may be very high.

● To call the US from Scotland dial 00 1, followed by the number. To call Scotland from the US, dial 011 44, then omit the 0 from the area code.

Language

Standard English is the official language of Scotland, and is spoken everywhere. However, as with other parts of Britain, the Scottish people have their own variations on the language and the way it is spoken. You should have no difficulty understanding the people of Edinburgh, who tend automatically to moderate their accent when speaking to non-Scots. But many Scottish words and phrases are used in everyday conversation.

COMMON WORDS AND PHRASES	
auld	old
awfy	very
aye/naw	yes/no
belong	come from
ben	hill, mountain
bide	live
birle	spin, turn
blether	to chatter, gossip
bonnie	pretty, attractive
braw	fine, good
burn	stream
canny	cunning, clever
ceilidh	party or dance
couthy	comfortable
douce	gentle and kind
dram	a measure of whisky
een	eyes
fash	bother
gae	go
gloaming	dusk
guttered	drunk
haar	sea mist
Hogmanay	New Year's Eve
ken	to know
kirk	church
lassie	girl
lum	chimney
messages	shopping
nicht	night
och	oh
Sassenach	non-Scottish person
trews	tartan trousers
wee	small

Timeline

EARLY SETTLERS

The area was first settled by hunting tribes around 3000BC and in about 1000BC the first farmers were joined by immigrant Beaker People, who introduced pottery and metalworking skills. Parts of Scotland were held by the Romans for a short time. After their departure in the 5th century AD the area suffered waves of invasion.

THE MACALPINS

Northumbrians held southern Scotland for 33 years, but were defeated in 1018 by MacAlpin king Malcolm II. Malcolm III married Margaret, sister of Edgar Atheling, heir to the English throne, but was usurped by William the Conqueror.

From left to right: Robert the Bruce statue; James VI of Scotland; the Forth Rail Bridge; posters for the Edinburgh Festival; Holyrood Park hosts Fringe Festival events

1314 Thomas Randolph retakes Edinburgh Castle from the English on behalf of Robert the Bruce.

1329 Edinburgh receives a Royal Charter from Robert the Bruce.

1349 Thirty percent of Edinburgh's population is killed by the Black Death plague.

1513 James IV is killed at the Battle of Flodden; work begins on Flodden Wall for the defence of Edinburgh.

1544 Edinburgh is attacked by English forces, who fail to take the city.

1566 Holyroodhouse is the scene of Darnley's grizzly murder of David Rizzio, the darling of Mary, Queen of Scots.

1603 James VI moves his Court to London after acceding to the English throne.

1633 Edinburgh officially becomes the capital city of Scotland.

1639 Parliament House is built and used by the Scottish Parliament until 1707.

1692–8 A run of bad harvests leads to riots.

1702–7 The Scottish Parliament debates and finally ratifies the Act of Union, voting itself out of existence.

1736 The Porteous Riots take place.

1767 First plans for New Town are adopted.

1817 *The Scotsman* newspaper is printed for the first time.

1824 The world's first municipal fire service is founded after fire rages in High Street.

1890 The Forth Rail Bridge opens.

1895 Electric street lighting is introduced.

1947 The first Edinburgh International Festival is held.

1970 The Commonwealth Pool and Meadowbank Stadium are built for the 1970 Commonwealth Games.

1971 St. James Centre opens. Further demolition of Georgian houses in Princes Street.

1986 The Commonwealth Games are held in Edinburgh for a second time.

1999 The Scottish Parliament sits for the first time since 1707.

2004 The Queen opens the striking new Parliament building.

2014 The referendum on Scottish Independence results in a "no" vote.

EDINBURGH'S FAMOUS

Some of Edinburgh's most famous citizens have had a significant impact on our lives. Alexander Graham Bell invented the telephone in 1847, and anaesthetics were pioneered by James Young Simpson. John Knox reformed Scotland's religion and architect Robert Adam and artists Henry Raeburn and Allan Ramsay brought their flair to the buildings of the city. The literary impact has been phenomenal, through the romances of Sir Walter Scott, who was born in the city in 1771, and the detective stories of Sir Arthur Conan Doyle. More fame comes from Robert Louis Stevenson, author of *Kidnapped* and *Treasure Island*, who was born here in 1850, and actor Sean Connery, who spent his early days here.

Index

INDEX

TITLES IN THE SERIES